Master Dressage

Peter Dove

DEDICATION

I'd like to dedicate this book to two of the most influential women in my life. Emma Dove, my wife, who keeps me grounded and focused on the important things in life and Mary Wanless for her inspiration and guidance in the riding, training and teaching of dressage.

CONTENTS

	Acknowledgments	i
	Foreword	iii
1	Introduction	1
2	Dressage	Pg 7
3	The System	Pg 11
4	Accuracy	Pg 19
5	Fluidity	Pg 61
6	Understanding	Pg 75
7	Practice	Pg 105
8	Review	Pg 133
9	Confidence	Pg 149
10	Rider Biomechanics	Pg 159
11	Physiotherapy	Pg 169
12	Your Next Steps	Pg 175
13	Your Questions	Pg 179
14	Learning Resources	Pg 187
15	Further Reading	Pg 191

ACKNOWLEDGEMENTS

I would like to acknowledge the positive effect in my life, riding and teaching of Mary Wanless BHSI BSC. Some of the ideas presented in this book came directly from Mary and have helped me develop a system for improving a riders' performance in dressage tests.

Peter Dove

FOREWORD

By

Mary Wanless BHSI BSc

Peter Dove has written about the principles of dressage and good competitive test riding, in a very accessible way that will benefit the many riders who either aspire to ride competitively, or who already do so at the lower levels. Even upper level riders will find great advice in this book.

I have known Peter for over twenty five years and have admired his smart, logical brain, that jibes unusually well with his feel and intuition. As well as being a rider and coach, he has played chess in international tournaments and is a maestro in computer programming. These skills combine a step-by-step understanding of the task with the vision of a desired long-term outcome, just as he has done in this book. (I, in contrast, have never even managed to learn the rules of chess!)

Peter has judged a huge number of lower level tests and has maintained the ability to perceive those tests and the challenges they present, from the viewpoint of a rider who struggles to perform well at those levels. He does not write as someone who thinks that these lower levels present so few challenges that they ought to be easy. He breaks down the various aspects of riding the test in helpful ways that you may not have thought of, starting with accuracy and fluidity. He then considers your understanding of the school movements, how you practice from day to day, and how you review your rides, both at home and after competition.

Peter describes the geometry of a test so well that if you do throw away marks through inaccuracy, it will not as a result of misunderstanding the pattern you should be riding! Sadly, almost all riders make the same mistakes when they ride corners, circles, diagonal lines, serpentines, etc., so judges see these again and again. Riding the movements accurately takes an understanding of the 'hows and whys' of the pattern you are riding, good riding skills, and focused concentration (or presence of mind). Skilled riders prepare the movements well, flow smoothly between them, and demonstrate the harmony between horse and rider that judges love to see.

Peter's practical guidelines include an introduction to my own field of rider biomechanics, which elucidates the 'how' of riding. Without this, you are more likely to make the same mistakes over and over again, even though you know that you *should* be getting a different result by now. With it, you are more likely to develop the skills that (for instance) prevent your horse from falling in or out through his shoulder and allow you to ride him on the line that is *your* choice, rather than his!

In your day-to-day training, it helps enormously to meld an understanding of the biomechanics of the rider/horse interaction with an understanding of the purpose of the school movements. How you practice at home has a huge bearing on whether or not you are able to improve your horse's carriage and movement, thus improving his 'ridability', his athleticism, and the scores your receive in your tests. But this can only happen if *you* improve too! Sadly, the power of the habits that would limit your learning (the lure of those same old mistakes) is very, very strong.

Peter helps to clarify how riding skills mesh with training skills, suggesting an approach to learning that also helps you to develop an appropriate, benevolent attitude towards your horse, yourself, and your riding. This honours the challenges you face and does not gloss over difficulties. It puts you and your horse on the same team and makes you a fair task-master. It enables both of you to benefit from step-by-step learning.

The school movements set a specific series of challenges both individually and in the many possible sequences that you might ride both at home and in competition. The way they are put together in a test are designed to demonstrate the strengths and weaknesses of your training to the judge. The feedback you receive on your test sheet can really help you plan your training, as can the feedback you are receiving from your horse in each moment, and within each ride as a whole. Few people work as well with this feedback as they could, mentally reviewing their rides and learning from them. Peter makes this easier, by helping you to improve your focus, and by giving you specific tools that have value for riders at all levels.

Read this book to help you understand and develop the skills that good trainers often take for granted. Students and teachers all benefit when these are made explicit, giving a road map that can take us from point A to point B. This is a journey of increasing skills and scores, designed to bring more satisfaction to your riding.

1 INTRODUCTION

More and more people are gravitating towards dressage; we are seeing a dramatic increase in the number of riders competing, training and looking for more specific information on how to get started with dressage. With eventing and jumping becoming more and more expensive, dressage is a cheaper and less stressful way to compete with your horse, especially for non-professional riders.

The difficulty facing most riders is that it is hard to know where to start with dressage competition. There are countless tests and numerous levels. In some centres they even make up their own tests!

In addition to understanding the judge's comments and how to apply those comments to their performance, competing at dressage requires the rider to understand the movements and how to perform them. In the past there has been little focus on the accuracy of riding tests, the mechanics of the movements, or what the judges are looking for in a well-ridden test. This is why I have written Master Dressage; this book has been designed to help people from the starting levels to elementary (2nd level US) for both unaffiliated(schooling shows) and affiliated level. However, even the higher levels, will benefit from the increased focus on accuracy and the training plans in this book.

The world of horse riding is changing.

People are no longer satisfied with vague instructions, the mystique of talented riders or the mishmash of teaching methods which seem to contradict each other and lack long-term effectiveness. Riders want answers! Riders today are becoming more intelligent about their training and are much more concerned with the welfare of the horse and using ethical training methods.

The new model of learning to ride and compete well is a holistic approach that covers such topics as rider biomechanics, the geometry and purpose of school movements, test riding, nutrition, saddlery, farriery and equine physiotherapy – just to name a few.

A rider now needs to have a strategy for improvement and competition so that they stay true to the horse and his welfare.

In terms of learning to ride tests, using school movements well and competing successfully, riders without a strategy and an overall understanding of the whole process will be left in the dark, wondering why they aren't improving and why their scores aren't going up. In fact, this can lead to the rider becoming disillusioned with the sport and even with their equine partner.

I was very lucky to be rescued from this confusion in my early 20s by an amazing coach, Mary Wanless – author of the *Ride With Your Mind* books and DVDs. I had become part of a culture which saw the horse as the antagonist and me as the victim – with the horse resisting my aids and evading work.

Before my awakening I never realised I was completely responsible for everything that happened! Mary taught me the psychology, the physiology and the tools to create profound change in myself and the horse. At the time of writing this book I am not a qualified RWYM coach, though all my coaching is based on RWYM ideas and techniques and it is a situation I intend to correct time willing!

In this You'll discover how to learn more effectively, how to develop a better relationship with your horse and how to develop an end-to-end strategy for training yourself and your horse to compete at dressage. I will show you the map, give you the right tools and be your guide to a more successful competitive experience.

One might ask how a book of this thickness could possibly help you 'master dressage', surely you would need a book of a thousand pages to do that? What I offer in these pages is a structured approach to improving your dressage that will allow you to make progress no matter where you are in your dressage learning. I would hope that after reading this book, you will know exactly what to do if you get stuck, have a better understanding of test riding and have a better relationship with your horse. You and your horse are on the same team, it should never degenerate into a 'him versus me'. In essence this book is in large part instruction in riding dressage but also is about teaching you how to learn more effectively.

Whilst this book contains plenty of how to information on riding movements, improving your training, solving training problems and getting higher marks, it is not an exhaustive manual for riding. So don't be too disappointed when you don't find detailed instruction on how to train your horse to do half-pass, or complex rider biomechanics to teach you to sit well, or the specifics of lungeing a horse. Such a scope as pointed out earlier would need a book ten times the size of this. Let me assure you though, there is lots of 'how to' but also lots of 'how to think' about dressage training and riding.

Each of the following chapters builds upon the chapter before it. Together they'll create an actionable framework for you to improve with an instructor and by yourself.

Chapter 2 covers the typical problems riders face as they attempt to learn dressage and then goes on to explain the new approach that is needed.

In Chapter 3 I give you the overall strategy I use to train riders to improve their marks. There are five steps you need to appreciate to have a successful approach to learning and riding and this chapter explains those steps.

In Chapter 4 we cover accuracy, the mechanics of the movements and where, people typically lose marks. This is a very important chapter as it will instill good habits in you, and you will develop the confidence to ride many different tests.

Chapter 5 addresses fluidity, which is how to string movements together, the ability to see ahead more than one movement and how to become aware of what needs to change from one movement to the next.

Once a rider has accuracy and fluidity, the next stage is understanding the purpose of the movements and the benefit they have. Chapter 6 will give you the confidence to enter the arena to train your horse knowing what you are doing. The solid base of fundamentals, strategy and knowing what you are trying to achieve will reduce the stress of the entire process on you and your horse.

Chapter 7 is about practice. Typically instructors expect riders to know what practice is and how to go about it. Practice requires a lot of responsibility and commitment from the rider. You will learn to practice perfectly for the sake of the horse and ultimately to develop consistency.

Finally in Chapter 8 we round out the last of the five steps with the review. To make sure you're making meaningful improvements you must regularly review your progress, benchmarking it against your goals and ideals and choose how to influence your practice, understanding, fluidity and accuracy going forward.

Chapter 9 is a about rider psychology and confidence in both training and competing by Jo Cooper of www.equestrianconfidence.com - This chapter will really help improve your confidence and help calm those nerves whilst competing.

Chapter 10 is an introduction to rider biomechanics by Mary Wanless BHSI BSc – www.mary-wanless.com. This chapter will help you develop greater balance and stability while riding.

Chapter 11 is a practical piece by Sue Palmer MCSP on Physiotherapy which your horse will really appreciate!

Chapter 12 recaps the system with the most important points, and gives you some next steps to begin immediately on the process of learning and improving for dressage.

Chapter 13 contains a list of questions and answers from my Facebook fans. I recently asked them for any dressage related questions they had, so I hope you find an answer in there for any questions you might have.

Chapter 14 gives some website links and coaches who can help with your training, learning and progress in dressage.

Chapter 15 is a reading list put together by myself. It's not the definitive list and I am sure I have left a lot of stellar texts off the list, however these are all worth reading.

Peter Dove

2 DRESSAGE

Dressage is more popular than it has ever been before.

There is an influx of riders at the lower levels and a abundance of competition types suitable for a new riders at the unaffiliated level.

The main problem facing riders wanting to start dressage though, is that there is still little information on test riding. Everywhere we look there are diagrams, describing the shapes but very little information on how to ride them well or what would get the rider a 7 or an 8 and so on in a dressage test.

Feedback on your progress is very difficult to get without spending lots of money on lessons and even feedback on test sheets is limited due to space. Also people seem left in the dark on how to approach schooling for dressage and there is little information provided on this even when riders have lessons. Instructors often assume a rider will know what to do when the pupil is by themselves in the arena with no instruction. In order to combat this, an overall strategy for streamlined progress is needed.

Despite the initial confusion, riders new to the dressage experience are seeing a number of improvements. More and more centres are putting on dressage, the science of rider biomechanics has advanced and riders are beginning to understand that the responsibility to change is theirs. Certainly dressage is now much more under the spotlight after Britain's success at the 2012 Olympics. To succeed a rider has to understand many different aspects including horse training, rider biomechanics, nutrition, psychology, physiology, and animal welfare.

For the average rider this means there is lots to learn. You are going to need a coherent plan, with actual steps you can take to get you from where you are now to where you want to be. One of the aims of this book is to be able to shine a light into all the different areas for improvement even though we are somewhat focused on school movements and test riding.

Faster improvements are there for the taking by riders who are willing to invest the time beyond the weekly lesson. It is no longer sufficient to ride your horse and then forget about your riding afterwards. You must be thinking and planning beyond the current lesson and have a responsibility to constantly improve. By developing discipline and a sense of responsibility to yourself and your horse you can take charge of your own destiny and find rapid improvement in both you and your horse.

Without a real determination to seek out new knowledge riders can find themselves frustrated with their horses, stuck on a learning plateau and losing interest in dressage. Without a holistic understanding of training and learning it's very easy to buy into the culture of blaming the horse for resisting or evading rather than accepting responsibility for the way things turn out.

Good riders and trainers accept responsibility for themselves and their horse, they read, seek out knowledge, find help and look inward and outward to improve. They apply what they've learned, they practice what they've learned and they review the results. When a rider commits to developing a rounded understanding of the entire sphere of horsemanship they find again their beginner's mind, the joy of learning and experience daily improvement.

My own learning came to a head early on in my career. I had become stuck on a plateau and laying the blame for it directly at the feet or hooves of my horse. My belief, backed by what other people were saying, was that my horse was evading me, my horse was resisting and my horse was avoiding doing work.

The saying goes that when the pupil is ready the teacher appears and luckily for me I found a coach who saved me and my horses. I began to start reading, exploring and questioning everything. Now 20 years on I study, practice, review, use mental rehearsal and treat my horses with respect and understanding. In the end it is often the horses that teach me!

I remember once being asked to school a mare and having a pretty bad ride the very first time I sat on her. At the end of the session I was exhausted and a little distressed at how poorly things were turning out. However that evening as I lay in bed I spent quite a lot of time in mental rehearsal replaying my previous ride and within a short space of time the solution had dawned upon me. It was one of those "Doh"! moments.

It occurred to me that on more experienced and balanced horses I am thinking about many things simultaneously. I am lifting the horse's back up, I am keeping it straight, keeping it reached out onto the end of the rein, maintaining impulsion and rhythm and so on. I realised that what had gone wrong on this less experienced horse was that I was trying to correct too many things at once. It was just too much for the mare. The very next day, when I schooled her again, I allowed her to be less straight. She remained rhythmical, round with reasonable impulsion and with a better contact on the rein. It turned out that by asking her to be straight was just one step too far for her. Things progressed much more quickly after that.

Within the chapters of this book I use photographs of my daughter, Milly, riding her part Welsh, part Thoroughbred mare Soley Magick Tinkerbelle. I use these photos, not because Milly is some super-skilled advanced rider on an advanced horse, but because she and the mare represent well the levels of intro/prelim/training. Milly is skillful enough to ride the pony in a nice outline, with a good tempo, a good level of energy and maintain the horses balance through it's shoulders. Milly is also skillful enough to do this without relying on her hands to make it all work. However she is not so skilled, that we are unable to pick faults in the photos. For me this is a really nice combination to help demonstrate points to the reader, but also be able to train the eye to spot other things to. When describing the photos I will also point out what could be improved.

3 THE SYSTEM

To pick up marks fast on your dressage score, I could simply teach you how to be more accurate. However this will be very limiting to your learning process. To give you the best chance of improvement, I have broken down my system into five sections and I will describe each one of them here briefly.

Accuracy

Becoming accurate isn't just a question of performing the movements at the right markers; the movements themselves must be performed accurately and one must present the horse in its best light. The need for accuracy when schooling your horse is often overlooked and because of this we often allow the horse to step and move inaccurately. At the lower levels, this is shown in cutting corners, drifting through the outside shoulder on circles, and lack of straightness on the centre line.

As you will see in the chapter on accuracy, inaccuracy can cause loss of balance and increased difficulty for your horse during the test. Riders can unwittingly lose marks because of the path they take around the arena. From another point of view, it is important to get into the habit of being accurate as until you know what accurate is, how do you know you have deviated from it? For instance, if you know the exact path of your circle you can more easily feel when you are losing control of the horse's shoulder.

In the chapter on accuracy I will show you typical errors that both horse and rider can make, the mechanics of the various school movements, ground-based strategies that can help improve your accuracy and also talk about the management of your horse's current capabilities.

As hinted at in the beginning of this chapter, accuracy is the quickest way to pick up marks that riders would otherwise typically lose and whilst you may think you're quite accurate, after reading the chapter I am sure you will see there is more to it. You will see that by improving your accuracy your horse will appear more balanced, more supple, and present a smoother test. Many of my pupils receive comments against the rider's marks along the lines of "well presented test" or "smoothly ridden". And if that isn't enough of an incentive, then just reflect on the fact that if you lost a single mark per movement due to inaccuracy then you would have lost approximately 6-8% from your marks - especially when you take the effect on your collectives. Why have a 62% test when you can have a 70% test?!

Fluidity

What is fluidity? Fluidity is how smoothly the horse changes bend and how smoothly it moves from one pace to another. It is how well the horse maintains its rhythm and tempo through movements and moves with a constant contact and outline. Fluidity is that easy grace which can make watching dressage a wonderful experience.

Fluidity is understanding where your horse is and where he needs to move to, in terms of body positioning, in terms of direction and in terms of gait/collection changes.

Another element of fluidity is preparation. Preparation can be something as simple as creating a slight bend before your turns, through to managing your horse's known issues and difficulties when going into a movement.

Fluidity can be achieved through practice. A typical movement that I like to practice, which can pick up a lot of marks, is the ability to move smoothly from medium walk to free walk on a long rein and back again to medium walk.

> **NOTE**
> Throughout this book 'Free Walk On A Long Rein'
> refers to the British Dressage definition of this
> movement. The USEF & FIDE version is called
> 'Stretching On A Long Rein'

Does your horse move smoothly from one gait to the next, can he remain in a consistent outline moving from walk to trot? In the chapter on fluidity I'll provide some tips which will help develop smoothness in transitions, smoothness in turns and ways of reducing obviousness of issues faced from performing a test.

A rider who has understood fluidity can help their horse maintain balance and create an air of competence during the test. The impression is of complete harmony between horse and rider. A rider who has understood fluidity tackles their test strategically, thinking not only movement by movement, but how the whole test fits together and how the movements will affect their horse.

When horse and rider perform the movements smoothly they gain marks, not only for each movement, but also in the collectives. The horse appears more supple, more obedient, more balanced and has greater harmony with the rider.

Understanding

Understanding what, you may ask? There is great benefit to understanding the purpose of the movements in a test. The movements in a test are put together to help demonstrate to the judge that your horse has reached a certain level of training. The marks you receive tell you how successfully you have trained your horse to that particular level.

By understanding the purpose of the movements, it will help you perform them better and it will assist you in structuring the training program for your horse more effectively. My instructor, Mary Wanless, often states that there are two toolkits that a rider can use. The first toolkit is your own body, in other words your position, your balance and the way you communicate with your horse. The second toolkit is the school movements. Providing that you are riding competently and have a good baseline in the first toolkit, riding the school movements correctly will help improve your horse's balance, suppleness and athleticism.

Understanding the school movements will give you a greater number of tools in your second toolkit. When schooling you will be able to choose the correct movement to perform next with your horse, to improve his balance or correct a fault. You will also have a better understanding of the 'levels of challenge' the different school movements possess and how that can affect and help structure the training of your horse. Let's say that your horse now easily performs a 20m circle; what do you do next? Do you perform a 15m circle, a 10m circle, a serpentine, or some other movement?

Practice

What is practice? Practice is essentially anything you are doing with your horse! You are always practicing something, everything you do counts, everything to do matters. Mary Wanless often says, practice makes perfect, not what you think you are practicing, but what you are actually practicing. What does this mean? It means that every time you allow your horse to fall out, he is practicing falling out and every time you make a smooth transition from walk to trot you are practicing and therefore getting better at making smooth transitions!

Good practice requires diligence; you are always

practicing. You should practice perfectly or at least strive to practice perfectly. I'm not saying one should never make mistakes, but rather I am saying that a rider should always be present in the moment and try to be aware of the consequences of what they are doing.

A typical example of this that I have seen in many tests, is that a rider has been told their horse must be 'off their leg'. This is not a bad thing, however riders can implement this to the exclusion of all else. I see horses move from walk to trot quickly but hollow while doing so. This horse may now be 'off the leg'; however the rider is practicing hollowing from walk to trot.

When is it okay to choose not to practice perfectly? Sometimes when training our horse, in order to make progress, we have to sacrifice a little perfection so that the horse does not feel overwhelmed or over-faced. For instance, I would always prefer the horse to make a smooth transition from walk to trot before asking it to make a quick transition. I choose to sacrifice the speed of the transition in order to produce a smooth one. Once the horse is making smooth transitions we can ask it to make them quicker.

The key point here really is the word 'choose'. The word implies, as previously mentioned, that we are aware of the consequences of what we are doing and are fully present from moment to moment. Many riders suffer from under-focus and many pieces of information about what is happening underneath them pass them by. A good analogy here is that of film. Moving pictures are made up of individual frames, all running past the projector at 25 frames per second; it's all happening so fast it looks smooth. This is what happens when you see a good rider, it all looks so easy and effortless, as if they are doing nothing. However their ability to focus from one moment to the next and feel the smallest changes underneath them, allows them to react quickly and subtly to the smallest errors. Without enough focus, a rider can be halfway around the circle before realising that they have lost their horse's shoulder.

In the chapter on practice I will give you some strategies to improve your focus, make your practice more efficient and try to give you a sense of how you would go about practicing for your tests. We will also talk a little bit about how to prepare your horse for competitions so that they experience less stress.

Review

Reviewing your work, your practice, and your competitive results will dramatically improve your progress. It is often very easy to get lost in the doing and miss important patterns and information which could be uncovered with more reflective thinking.

In the chapter on review I provide several tools which will help you understand where you are at with your training and how you can spot errors that you would have otherwise missed without a conscious review process.

It is very easy to visit your horse, ride for your allotted time and then forget about the whole thing till next time you ride, especially whilst attempting to hold down a full-time job or with countless other sources vying for your attention.

Many of my breakthroughs, both in my own skill set and in overcoming a training hurdle with a horse, have come through review sessions after I have ridden. One can use mental rehearsal, watch a video, keep a diary, ask friends or even create a spreadsheet for competition results.

Without such a review, it would be very easy to turn up to the next training session ready to 'do battle' with the 'difficult horse'.

As the supposedly more intelligent being it is up to us to 'figure it out'. It is not up to the horse to become a good boy, or learn his lessons, or stop being such a brute. The responsibility for how well the horse goes, or at least the vast majority of it lies with us. If you ever find yourself saying "if only my horse would just..." then it's time to do a review of your riding, tactics and strategy. This review could come in the form of coaching or help from a more experienced rider.

And Finally...

Getting better at dressage and improving your score, from reading the above, may seem like a lot of work. This is in fact why a lot of people don't make the progress they want, because of the complexity of the task. Rather than being overwhelmed, we simply start from the beginning taking what steps we can, one at a time. At the end of the book you will find a section on which steps you should take next to get immediate results. The easiest to implement will be the section on accuracy. This is why it is first; without accuracy all the other stages will get undermined.

4 ACCURACY

As mentioned in the previous chapter, accuracy is probably the quickest way to pick up, or at least not throw away marks in a dressage test. However, it is not the act of being accurate which brings in the extra marks, the mere fact of learning to be more accurate allows your horse to become more balanced and have the greatest chance of performing well in the test. It is the benefits of being accurate which increase your marks too.

Comments from the judge such as "needs more suppleness" or "needs better balance" may stem from the fact that the movements were performed in a manner which made both requirements difficult for the horse to fulfill. In this chapter I will cover the typical movements required in a dressage test and the best way to approach learning them, performing them and developing accuracy which will get the extra marks in your test.

Lets first consider the arena itself and for the vast majority of this chapter I will talk about the 20m x 40m arena. Towards the end of the chapter, I will briefly discuss the 20m x 60m arena and some of the additional letters and measurements there. Most of the advice I give for the 20m x 40m will work just as well in the 20m x 60m.

Take a look at diagram 1. This is of a 20m x 40m arena. Let's talk about some of the more salient points of this arena size and the letters around it.

The line A to C splits the arena in half down the length, The line E to B splits the arena in half along the width. The centre of the arena is marked by the letter X. The other markers, HM and KF, connect as shown in the diagram, to produce some further letters on the centre line G and D. H,M,K and F are all 6m in from the ends of the arena.

As we progress through this chapter I will add in some additional lines to this diagram to help illustrate different points. We will be covering the following:

- Accurate 20m circles.
- How to ride corners.
- Riding up the centre line.
- How to approach turns.
- Change the rein across the diagonal.
- Riding 15m circles at different markers.
- Changing the rein through two half 10m circles.
- Half 10m circles and incline back to the track.
- 3 loop serpentines.
- Loops 5m and 10m in from the track.
- Transitions.
- 20m x 60m differences and the arena letters.
- The role of rhythm in balance and accuracy.

20M x 40M Arena

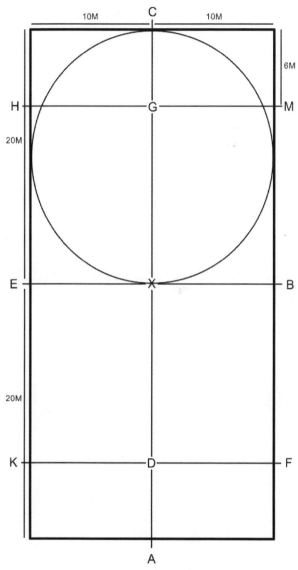

Diagram 1

20m Circles at A & C.

I thought we would start with 20m circles as the basic unit of a dressage test. Especially since, over all the time I have been judging, this is the thing I see done most incorrectly by the majority of people. In diagram 2, I have placed two 20m circles, one at C and one at A.

The 20m circle at C is obviously the correct version of the circle. Lets have a look at the characteristics of the circle within the arena.

- It touches the track in only 3 places
- It goes through X
- It does not go into any of the corners!

There are a couple of things we can think about which will help us perform a good circle. Firstly if we start the circle at C, we are stepping off the track at C. We do not continue along the wall and we do not go anywhere near the corners. In fact, we only touch the track again on the long sides at half way between the C end and the X end. I have circled these points with small dotted circles.

Some of the typical errors in riding 20m circles at A & C are shown in the 'circle' drawn at A. Riders tend to continue on the track past the A marker, instead of stepping off at that point. Riders then do a version of riding into the corner, then along the long side, before realizing they should be turning. After that point it's usually a drift across the school.

Drifting on circles is a really common error, even if a rider manages to understand that they must not go into the corners and that the circle has only 3 touch points on the track. Often it's the final part of the circle which goes through X where riders lose accuracy. It helps to think that X is the high point of the curve and that the moment you are stepping on X, you must be turning away from it.

20m Circles at C and A

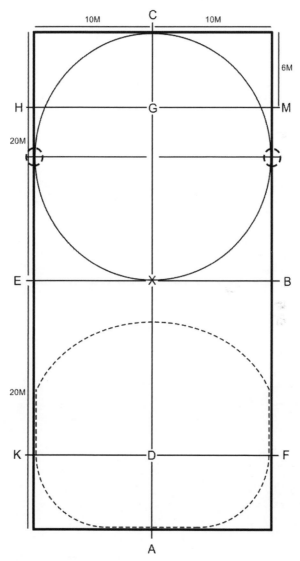

Diagram 2

It's important to think of a circle as a continuous turn and at no point on the circle should you be on auto-pilot drifting around. Mary Wanless, author of the Ride With Your Mind books and DVDs, describes it this way:

"Imagine you are trotting on top of a gymnastic balance beam, raised off the floor, which is just wide enough for your horse. This balance beam is bent into the perfect 20m circle shape. Your job is to make sure your horse trots on top of the balance beam and does not fall off".

If you were indeed trotting along the top of this balance beam, you would be very sure you kept turning and didn't drift off one side or the other. You can also use this piece of imagery to ask yourself 'which side of the balance beam would I fall off?' – would it be to the inside or to the outside? By frequently asking yourself this question, you will become a lot more accurate and a lot more aware of the deviations your horse may be making.

Falling out, with too much inside bend, is a much more frequent error and often completely by-passes the rider's radar for straightness problems. This is because falling in is much more obvious. When the horse is falling out riders are often lulled into a false sense of security believing they have a nice inside bend in the neck. The balance beam idea, is a great litmus test, since it won't allow falling onto either shoulder.

To become really good at circles and develop your accuracy, you need to be much more picky about where your horse's shoulders are in relation to the circle. You need to develop that wonderful feel of a horse which is equally weighted through both shoulders even on the most challenging of turns and circles.

Photo 1

Photo 1 is of my daughter warming up her pony at a British Dressage competition at one of the first outings we went on with the mare.

I include it here because I think it amply demonstrates the amount of inside bend needed for a 20m circle. It is only a small amount of inside bend and you should notice that the horse is free through its inside shoulder.

Too much inside bend and not enough balance through the shoulders can lead to the horse being restricted through the inside shoulder and heavily weighted on the outside shoulder. If we apply the visualization here of trotting along the top of a balance beam, the mare would stay there without a problem.

20m Circles at E & B.

In diagram 3 you can see a correctly shaped 20m circle. This circle reaches 10m either side of X. You can see the 10m radius line drawn in for clarity.

If there was a circle known for drifting horses and riders, it is this one. Typically the judge sees a rather deep first half of the circle and a somewhat shallow second half.

The best way to approach the circles at E and B is to split it into quarters and ride each section. For illustrative purposes let us imagine we are on the right rein and that we have to do a circle at E. First, as noted for all circles, we should be turning away from the track at E and we are aiming for the point on the centre line which the circle crosses through. As you approach the centre line, you then need to be looking across at B, remembering that you will spend only a short time at the B marker. As you approach B, look across again to the centre line where the circle will cross it. Finally on reaching the centre line again you should be looking at E.

A real give away for judges, for circles at E and B, is when the rider leaves the track before/after the marker and finishes before/after the marker. If the rider is performing any straight lines at E or B whilst on the circle, it's a sure sign of falling out on the circle. When getting to the marker at E or B, your horse's shoulder should hit the track a smidge before B or E.

One idea, which I use a lot for turns, is that you should have a really good idea at what angle you come away from the track, for any given turn or circle. How sharply must you turn away from the wall for a 20m circle, or a 10m circle? Knowing this will give you a good chance of beginning your circle accurately.

20m Circles at E and B

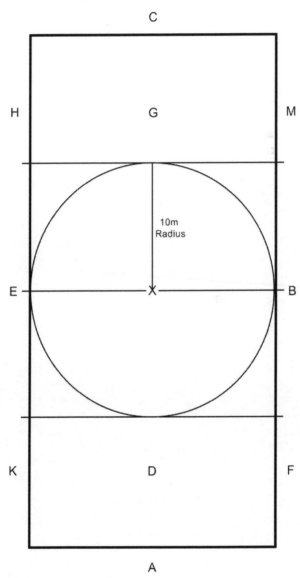

Diagram 3

Corners.

In diagram 4 you can see four different sizes of circles, placed into the arena ranging from 20m to 6m. What do all of these circles have to do with corners? You can see that the circles are all clearly placed as close to a corner as possible, the 20m circle covers two corners.

One way to think about corners would be to simply ride into them as deeply as possible. Another way, one which I believe will give you the highest chance of earning more marks, is to treat a corner as a quarter circle.

Photo 2

Photo 2 shows Milly riding 'into' the corner in walk. You can see the horse has a bend to the inside and still looks balanced though both of its shoulders.

Corners

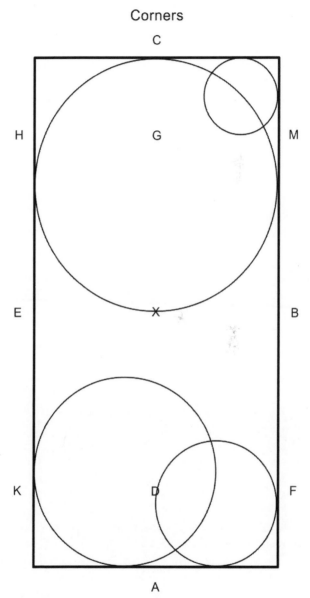

Diagram 4

Whenever I ride, I know, for each pace, how large a radius of quarter circle I am going to ride, in each corner. To not have a good idea of this, for your horse, is to practice your corners inconsistently and risk falling in or falling out on your turns. By being as clear as possible how you are riding the corner, you will be making sure the horse stays as balanced as possible through its shoulders, through the turn.

The radius of your quarter circle will change, depending on the pace and possibly depending on whether you are schooling at home, or out competing. At a competition you may want to choose a larger radius than the one you are challenging your horse's balance with at home.

As mentioned already, pushing your horse into the corner is most likely to lead to the horse falling out through its shoulder and losing balance. Done correctly corners are an excellent way to develop balance and challenging the horse in incremental ways under your control. Teach your horse even balance through both shoulders, gradually decreasing the radius of the quarter circle. Corners are a 'school movement' that you will use again and again, building up those repetitions of balance on turns.

Remember to use the imagery of the balance beam, even for the quarter radius circle, to gauge how balanced and accurate you are.

Riding accurate corners also helps remove that feeling when you get to competitions, that the corners come up too quickly and you find yourself winging around them. You will see a corner, know the radius of the circle and begin your turn. Have a look at the 10m circle in the AF corner. You would be approaching this, possibly in trot, and treat it as if someone had said "Just after F circle right 10m diameter. Except of course you only do a quarter of it. If you ride all your corners like this, you will never find yourself pulling on the inside rein attempting to make it around the corner.

You may initially find that the corners feel really bad, that the horse comes off the track or that you can't get it consistently. Stick with it, in my experience it doesn't take many repetitions for both you and your horse to learn the appropriate radius for the pace you are in. Remember if you have been doing corners by pushing the horse onto the outside shoulder, you will both have developed a habit and that habit may take a little while to change.

Keep working at it patiently remembering that this will be different for the horse too. The main key here is how well can you stay focused. Are you able to do every corner like this? How often do you zone out and forget to ride the corner properly? Pay attention when you do movements like change the rein across the diagonal, as it is easy to slip into the habit of pushing deep into the corner once you make it to the opposite side.

If you are at the intro level then you will probably find corners in canter very difficult, and I think it's the biggest mistake I see in canter even up into the higher levels. Just choose a bigger radius of circle and work on keeping the shoulders level.

Riding up the centre line.

In diagram 5, at the A end, you can see two curves joining the short end of the arena to the centre line. These curves were taken from a 10m and a 6m circle. There are a number of tips I can offer to get you onto the centre line and straight.

Choose the distance from the letter A you wish to start your turn. In effect we are choosing the radius of the quarter circle for the turn. Choose a radius that you know your horse can make and stick to it for a while at least.

Learn the angle at which you must leave the track for the radius you have chosen. This will give you the best chance to hit the centre line. This will take some practice.

Once you leave the track, make sure you keep your eyes on C and be prepared to keep making small adjustments to get your horse straight onto the centre line. And KEEP turning… remember there should never be any drift, you are making a conscious turn, just the same as a corner. Once more think about the balance beam on the turn. Your horse should step the path of the quarter circle equally balanced through both shoulders. If you are finding it difficult to make the turn, choose an easier radius. The horizontal bars on the centre line in diagram 5, mark where the curve meets the centre line. If you can correctly complete your turn at the marker, you will be set up to be straight – keeping the C marker between your horse's ears.

If you find yourself wobbling on the centre line, it is likely you have overshot by allowing your horse to drift and not completing the turn or you have undershot by not choosing the appropriate radius or distance from the A marker.

After making it onto the centre line we have to turn left or right. Whichever turn you are making, we face the same decision, we have to decide the radius of the quarter circle we will use as the turn.

Center Line

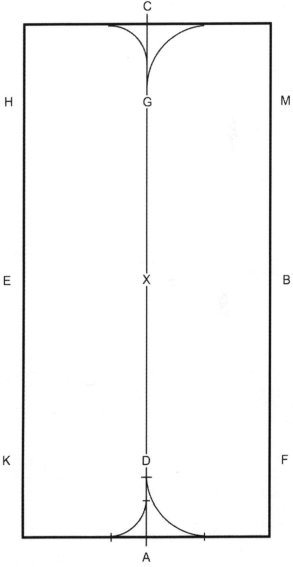

Diagram 5

Approaching turns.

In diagram 6, I have added in some curves for turns at E and B. If you have been paying attention to the previous discussions you will realise I am about to start talking about quarter turns!

The same lessons we have learned about corners, circles, and the centre line can be applied as easily to turns. Lets just recap the main points:

1. Choose the radius of the quarter circle for the turn.
2. Know the distance from the marker to start your turn.
3. Think of the balance beam as you turn to keep smooth control of the shoulders.
4. Never drift, keep turning until it is complete.
5. Keep your eye on the marker you are turning to. If you turn left at E, after you start the turn, keep your eye on B.

Some further tips for turning, come in the section on fluidity, however I can say you should have a very slight bend to the inside even when going large. This certainly helps improve the suppleness of your horse, but it also makes starting your turns and circles far easier. You should of course be totally straight in movements which require it, such as up the centre line etc.

Turns

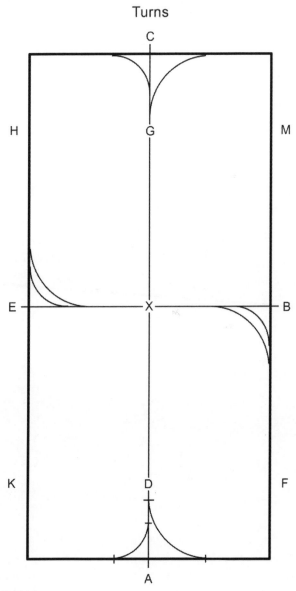

Diagram 6

Changing the rein across the diagonal.

In diagram 7, I have added in two changes of rein, namely FXH and MXK. The difference between the two is in the radius of the corner chosen by the rider. FXH chooses a smaller radius, which is more into the corner, than MXK.

The reason for adding in both was to highlight the fact that there is a small amount of straightness, as you come out of the corner, before you leave the track at F or M (assuming we are riding it FXH or MXK). This is important to realise, since some riders come hurtling out of the corner and immediately turn.

Photo 3

In the above photo Milly is changing the rein KXM and is almost at M. In fact in this photo M is the vertical metal beam slightly ahead of Milly. When the horse gets onto the track Milly's shoulder will be at M and she will be ready to ride around her corner after a slight moment of straightness. A quick note, she should have changed her stick into the other hand before this point.

To be really accurate think of riding your corner as already outlined and then have the horse's inside foreleg step off the track at, or very slightly before F or M, so that his outside shoulder peels away from the wall at the marker. Thinking this way will produce the smoothest turn and it's certainly less difficult for the horse than 'winging out of the corner'.

Photo 4

In the above photo you can see Milly making the turn onto the KXM change of rein across the diagonal. She is looking up for her M marker and you can see the horse is making the first step away from the track with a slight bend to the right. She is a little deep in the outline due to a loss of impulsion out of the corner. Always something to work on! I hope you could spot that too – you can see that the horse won't be tracking up fully.

However, we are only half way there! One of the ways

in which mistakes are made is with the arrival at the other side, in our example at H or K. Riders often end up cutting corners, or moving in an unbalanced way around the corners. Have a look at the diagram and notice that I have placed a couple of arrows just before M and just before H. It is my recommendation that you aim your horse's nose at these points, about half a horse's distance before the marker, so that as you hit the track at H or M, your horse's shoulder will be on the track exactly at the marker.

By aiming slightly before the marker you are helping improve the situation caused by the fact that you are riding a long vehicle! If the nose touches the track at H or M, then the body won't hit the track until after those markers and by then the corner is coming up. Aim slightly before and you will find you go more smoothly into the corner with less of a sharp turn for the horse to make.

Change of Rein Across Diagonal

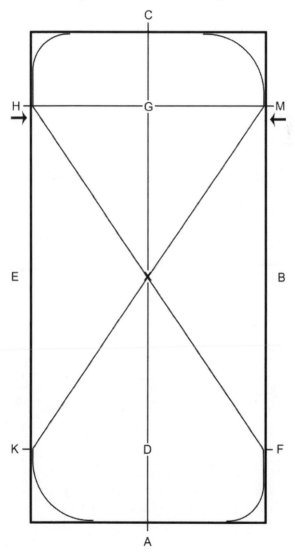

Diagram 7

15m Circles.

In diagram 8, I have added in two 15m circles. 15m circles are pretty tricky to ride accurately. The circle at C has only 2.5m in from the track either side at its widest point and 5m in from X. The widest point of the circle is 7.5m away from the C end, which is actually only 1.5m down from H and M.

All our previous discussions on circles and turns apply to this circle:

- Learn the angle you need to leave the track.
- Know the 'points' in the arena you have to hit.
- Keep turning, do not drift.

In addition to the above points, I think it's time to suggest a fun exercise! Find yourself a lunge line, a measuring tape and some means of marking the lunge line. I tend to use a small amount of electrical tape.

Measure out 7.5m on the lunge line and mark the length off with some tape, then have one person stand at C and the other person on the centre line with the lunge line at its 7.5m length. Then the person at C can start tracing a circle around the person standing on the centre line. In most surfaces, the person describing the shape can simply drag their feet into the surface and produce a very accurate circle.

By drawing in the 15m circle at C you will get a good sense of the angle at which you need to leave the track and how wide the circle is.

The 15m circle at B or E is so difficult for people to see, that it really does pay to draw the circle into the school arena. The main issue that people have with the circle at E or B is that 7.5m either side of the E/B line doesn't really come near any convenient markers and its difficult to split the circle into quarters like the 20m circle. The most recognisable point on the 15m circle at E/B is, in fact, the three quarter line, which is the furthest the circle reaches.

15m Circles

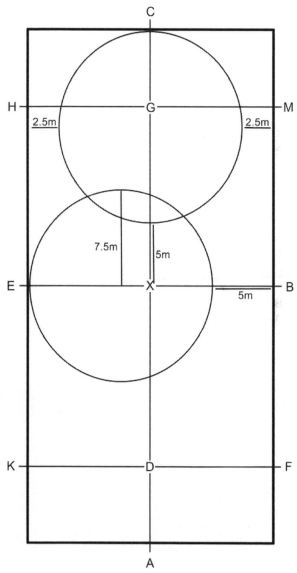

Diagram 8

3 Loop Serpentines.

Three loop serpentines are pretty tricky to work out, so let me break this down. The loops are actually 13.3M half circles joined by a straight line. The straight line is actually pretty short and crucial to riding these serpentines well.

Have a look at diagram 9 to see the three half 13.3M circles. Notice the straight line joining them. Other things to notice are that if we started on the left rein at C, then the first loop ends up on the centre line approximately between M and B. Its actually slightly to the right of that mid-point but it's a good visual aid as you turn away from the track just after H. Again when you turn away from B you can look across to approximately between E and K to hit the centre line.

There is a knack to riding a three loop serpentine well, and I personally love riding them. To help you out, I will give you a few tips.

- Treat them correctly as half circles joined by a short straight section.
- Use the straight section to change you diagonal if you are in rising/posting trot and to change the bend.
- Take your time to make a smooth change of bend, you have a number of steps to achieve this.
- Begin your change of diagonal before you get to the centre line. Remember that you sit for two beats and will travel some distance when changing your diagonal. If you wait until the centre line, you will still be changing your diagonal when you are meant to be changing your bend and moving onto the next half circle.

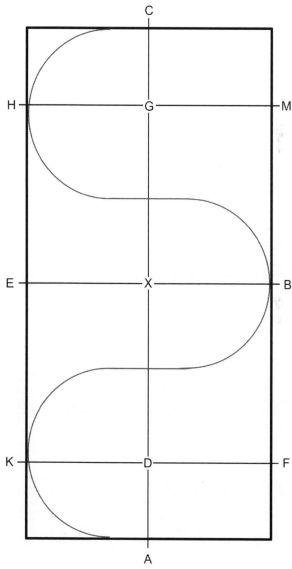

Diagram 9

- Make sure that as you come to change your diagonal you are straightening up your horse.
- As you come up out of the change of diagonal change the bend of your horse to the new circle.
- Always try to make your change of diagonal very smooth, stay responsible for your own weight on the sit so as not to cause the horse to hollow.

One of the movements you should work on first before the three loop serpentine is changing the rein through two half 20m circles. This will get you used to changing the bend and changing the diagonal. You need to get your horse used to changing the diagonal without upsetting his balance and shape of his back. This requires you to be responsible for your own weight as you double sit.

What is the judge looking for? Smooth changes of bend, that the horse maintains its tempo through the changes of bend and that the horse maintains its level of impulsion. The horse should remain consistently reached into the rein and maintain its focus on the rider.

I have added in the diagram opposite, the change of rein through two half 20m circles. Actually, in terms of changing bend, the speed with which you must change the bend in the two half 20m circles is faster but less severe, but you might want to adjust the circles a little bit to give you a closer experience to that of the serpentines, simply to get your horse used to this change of bend & change of diagonal.

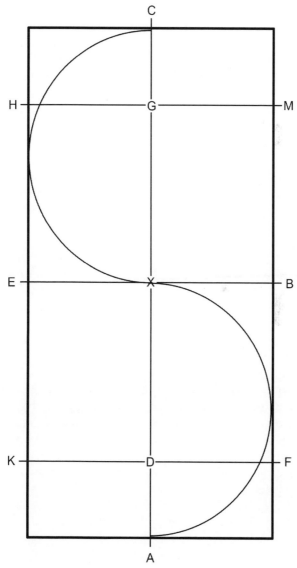

Diagram 10

10m Circles.

In diagram 11, there are 10m circles in several places. We can look firstly at the ones at E and B. You can see I have added the 5m radius line in against the circle and the dashed line is the most frequent mistake I see riders make, by making this circle too deep.

The only real way to get good at 10m circles is to draw them into the arena floor using the method I have already explained. You need to learn the angle at which you come away from the track and really keep your eye on the markers as much as possible. If you are doing a circle at B you will come away from the track at the angle you have learned from experience and then as quickly as you can keep an eye on X. As you then approach X you will need to start looking again at B.

All the time you should be thinking about the balance beam and continually turning. Be careful not to create too much bend, as your horse will tend to fall onto his outside shoulder. As stated before, your horse turns using his shoulders – so keep his shoulders on the ideal path.

10m Circles at A and C are harder even than at E or B. At least at E/B you have two clear touch points, the marker and the centre line. If you are familiar with doing lateral movements from the three quarter line, you can at least know that's how far you must come out on the circle. I have marked into the diagram the ¾ line and you can see this is 5m either side of the centre line. You will finally cross the centre line, half way between A and X. After drawing the circle into the school floor you will be able to train your eye.

Drawing the circles into the school floor is like having training wheels and after a while you might just want to mark out the quarter points of the circle. You could have two versions of the circle marked into the school floor, full circle and one with just quarter points marked.

10m Circles

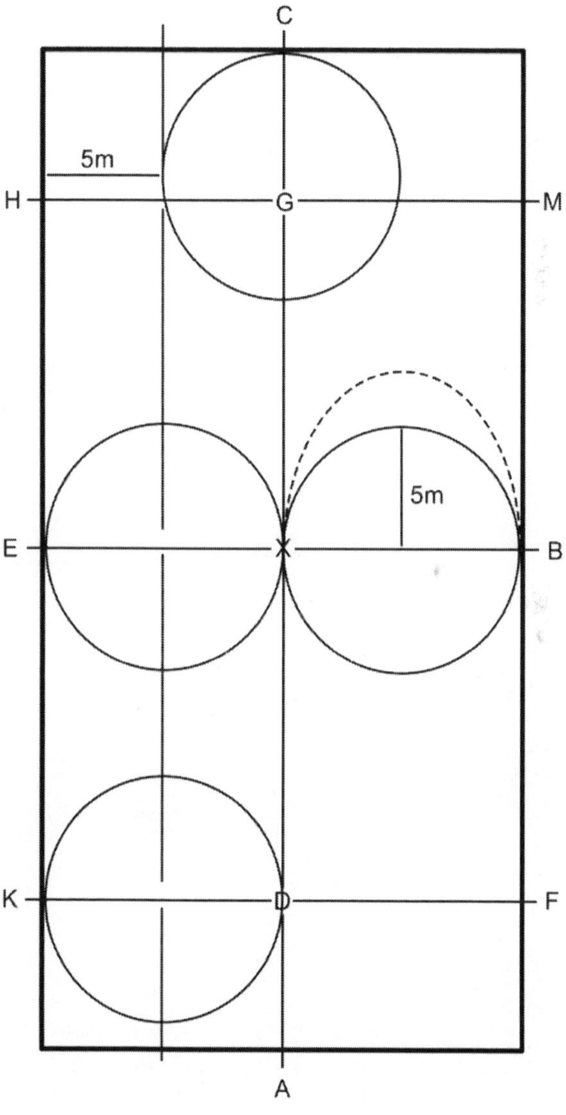

Diagram 11

Change rein through two half 10m circles.

As we go through the levels we are asked to change the rein through two half 10m circles. The tests ask for it in walk, then in trot, then in canter with a simple change through X.

Typical mistakes, in the change of rein through two half 10m circles, are:

- Riders makes the 1st circle too deep.
- Spending too long straight on the centre line.
- Not stepping off the track at first marker (E/B).

Most often, when judging tests, I see riders making loops instead of half circles. This makes the angles much sharper than needed and is almost guaranteed to lose balance. An example of the loop shape I most often see is added as a dotted line at B in the previous diagram. Once again it's definitely worth getting out the lunge line and drawing the circle out on the school floor, or at the very least marking a 5m line either side of B.

The biggest challenge for riders is changing the bend through X. Here is what British Dressage have to say about this kind of movement:

"The athlete should make his horse straight an instant before changing direction at the centre of the figure".

Now don't let this statement have you make violent or hasty changes of bend, however it should make it clear that you are not on the centre line for many strides. If you do find yourself dwelling on the centre line for more than a horse's length, check out the depth of your circle. Have a look at the diagram and you can see that the circles touch only briefly and if you draw them out on the arena floor you can see that clearly.

10m Circles

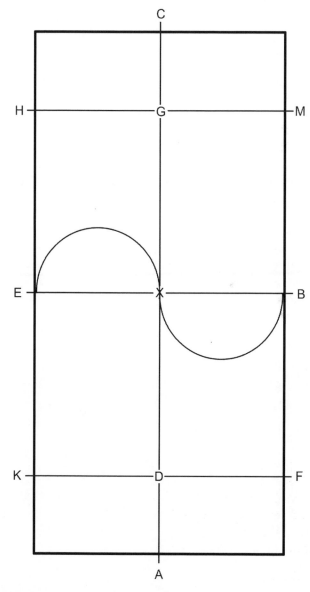

Diagram 12

Angles of attack.

In certain movements, such as half-circle then incline back to the track, we are to hit the track at a certain angle and then go large. It is the rider's responsibility to think about the angle with which we are going to hit the track.

The shallowest angle of attack will give us the least difficult for the horse. As an example I was judging Novice 28 and one movement was "just before H half circle 15m diameter and incline back to the track between E & K"

I saw so many people during that test starting their half 15M circle well before H and giving themselves such a hard task! Have a look at the diagram opposite. Notice that the line from the half 15m circle to the K marker is less steep the closer to H you do the 15m half circle. What that means is your horse doesn't have to make such a sharp turn onto the track and can appear more balanced.

So why not do it at H? Well for a start the directive is 'just before H'. But the main reason is that H is only 6 meters in from the track, and a half 15m circle needs you to start 7.5 meters in from the end.

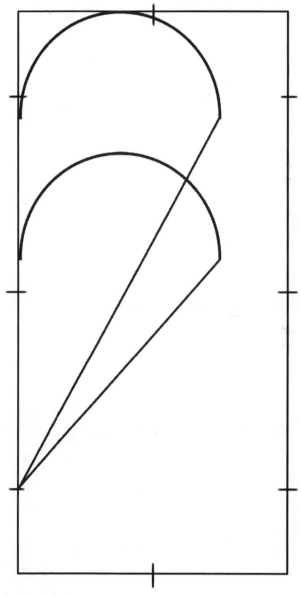

Diagram 13

Angles of inaccuracy.

I remember writing for a judge in an advanced medium and watched quite a few horses come in and out. One error which caught my eye a lot was the 10m circle. We often had horses falling out and then, upon getting back onto the track, made a second error of balance.

To illustrate what I mean more clearly, have a look at diagram 14 opposite. On the right you will see a correctly shaped 10m circle and the line you see from it is an attempt to show the angle of the horses body as it steps onto the track. The horse hits the track with a fairly shallow angle.

The circle on the left shows what happens when the rider loses control of the shoulder and drifts on the second half of the circle. You can then see the mistake I saw numerous times in the test, where the horse has to make a much sharper turn to the right to get back onto the track again.

So not only did the rider get a mark off for falling out through shoulder, but they lost another mark for loss of balance onto the track again. No doubt they will have lost some fraction of a mark too for their overall collectives, if they repeated the error elsewhere.

I am sure if the riders were aware of the balance beam and used it in all their training, then they would not make this mistake in their competition. This kind of error is often made when we fall into the trap of over bending to the inside.

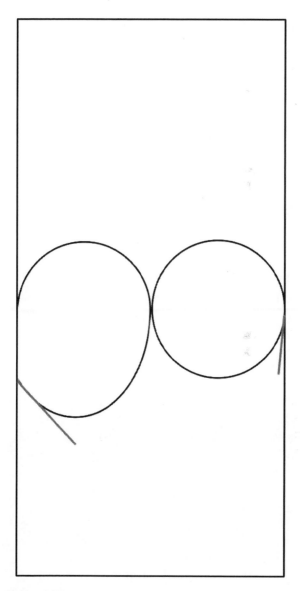

Diagram 14

The 20m by 60m arena.

Everything you have learned regarding the school shapes will also work just as well in the 20m x 60m arena. I hope in the preceding pages I have given you the bug for accuracy and given you enough information to extrapolate out to the larger arena size.

Looking at diagram 15 you can see that we can now fit in three 20m circles. Unfortunately we no longer have the luxury of X as our marker for circles at A and C. A circle of 20m at A comes 2m above the VLP line and this is something you should probably mark out on your arena to get the feel for the distance. I put small dotted circles to mark out the 2m distance.

HM & FK are still 6m in from the end of the arena. The remain distances between the horizontal lines made by HGM, SIR, EXB, VLP and KDF are 12m apart. A quick bit of maths is 4 x 12m sections and the 2 x 6m sections comes to 60m.

For our US cousins the 20m x 60m arena is the norm, but here in the UK we spend quite a bit of time in the 20m x 40m arenas which makes 20m x 60m seem a little daunting! Hopefully some study of diagram 15 will allow you to set out some markers and get used to the few differences there are.

The main challenges I find are that it is harder to keep your horse straight when it counts. The centre lines are much longer, as are changes of rein. The other issue can be balance in canter, as we have a much longer side to canter down before we have a corner we can use for balance.

When schooling in the longer arena make frequent use of circles to keep the horse balanced and maintaining attention. I often joke with pupils that when I allow them off circles and to start going large around the arena, they have grown up and can now be trusted to hold a horses attention!

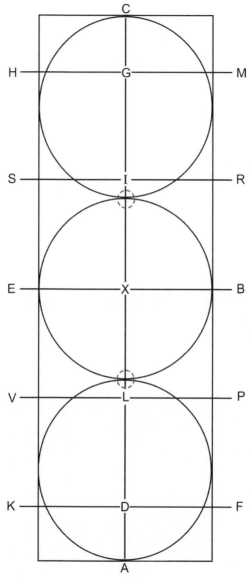

Diagram 15

Transitions

Transitions should occur at the marker and you will be penalised for being early or late. To be even more exact, the transition should occur as your shoulder is at the marker. For instance, if we were to halt at A, and the letter A was on the wall at shoulder height, then the judge at C would not see the letter any more, since it would be obscured by your own body.

It pays to know how long it takes for you to make your upward and downward transitions and practice being accurate when you make them. My view is that I first want to teach a horse how to make a smooth transition and then increase how quickly it can do it. I can still be accurate, I just have to know how long my horse will take to make the transition.

5m and 10m loops in from the track

To help us understand this movement I am going to take us on a ride through of a 10m loop in from the track between H and K on the left rein in trot. This movement is meant to be performed as a series of smoothly joining curves showing several changes of bend.

As I trot past C I create an appropriate bend of the radius of ¼ circle I need to get around the corner. Approaching H I create a left bend and look to X. I leave the track at H. About halfway between H and X, I begin to straighten the horse and then change bend smoothly to the right. The plan is to smoothly approach X with a right bend and treat it like a shallow curve with the apex at X.

As I reach X I am now looking across at K and make my way to K, aiming my horse slightly before the K marker. As I get halfway between X and K, I begin to straighten my horse and then smoothly change the bend to the left. I hit the track at K in a left bend and ride the corner.

In the 10m loop on the left rein from H to K there is a smooth curve to the left from H to half way between H and X. This changes into a smooth curve to the right between that half way point to X. The right bend is maintained to half way between X and K. Half way between X and K the bend smoothly changes to a left bend all the way to K. Check out the website in the near future and we should have more diagrams available.

The role of rhythm in balance and accuracy.

British Dressage has Rhythm as the basis of the scales of training. Outside of dressage, rhythm can be defined as, a movement or procedure with a uniform or a patterned recurrence of a beat.

This definition says nothing about tempo, and generally speaking when the horse loses balance we often see a change in the tempo, rather than a loss of rhythm. In the detailed comments in the scales of training material, reference is made to tempo. Comments based on rhythm are more congruent with a horse becoming tense, perhaps the walk sequence breaking, or the horse becoming unlevel in its steps.

Having tempo control is extremely important and without it your progress in dressage is almost impossible. Why is tempo control so important? Generally horses take the path of least resistance, so should we apply our leg, the horse will choose to speed up the tempo first of all. We must have a way of saying 'no, not faster, but more energy' or 'no, not faster, but move sideways' or 'no, not faster, but lengthen your stride'. All of these imply control of tempo and so rhythm (and tempo) is placed as most important in the scales of training.

With reference to accuracy, I tend to talk a lot about having control of your horse's shoulder. For this to happen and particularly when it comes to correcting a horse which has fallen onto one shoulder or the other, one must have tempo control. Without it your corrections will not straighten the horse, who will most likely continue falling out, and simply speed up its tempo.

Creating school shapes

Training a horse is such great fun and involves so many diverse skills and exercises other than just going round in circles, it can really keep us busy! I have already mentioned drawing shapes, but thought a little more detail will help.

For this you will need the following items:

1. A lunge line longer than 10m
2. A measuring tape or measuring stick.
3. Coloured electrical tape.
4. A good humored helper.

The purpose of this fun exercise is to draw upon the school floor the circles, turns and corners that we want to learn and become more accurate whilst performing.

For a 20m circle, mark on the lunge line the point of 10m by putting some electrical tape around it at the 10m point. Let's take a 20m circle at the letter C. Your helper will be holding on to the end of the lunge line, so have them stand at C. You should then walk backwards down the centre line until the lunge line is taut and you are holding it at the tape line you marked. Now with you spinning on the spot, your helper should walk around you, dragging her feet in the arena sand, whilst keeping the lunge line taut. Once your helper has gone around you twice, you should have a near perfect 20m circle etched into the surface if your arena.

Actually, as an aside, I should mention that you should probably measure out your arena to be sure of its dimensions. Indoor arenas seem to vary in size quite a lot depending on how they are constructed. Our arena is wider than 20m so we have to put out boards on competition days to narrow it slightly.

Now you know the 'secret' you can do this for 10m circles too. Measure out a 5m length on the lunge line and repeat the same procedure as before. 15m circle should be a 7.5m length of lunge line.

Photo 5

The above photo isn't great quality, but hopefully you can see Milly at the end of a lunge line and she is walking around me dragging her feet in the ground. I also drew in the circles too to make them clearer.

Corners are a little bit trickier but they are well worth drawing into the arena floor. Firstly you should look at my diagram on corners earlier in the chapter. It's probably worth doing a 6m corner, a 10m corner, a 15m circle and then just using the 20m circle as the corner too. With this range of corners set up you can try each of them in each of the paces and decide what fits your horse best. You may find that some in between radius is better.

The best way to do a corner circle is to have yourself stand right into the corner. Your helper then moves along the short side until the lunge line is taut. Once your helper is stationary you can move out of the corner keeping the lunge line taut, and standing at 90 degrees to the short side.

Once this is done and with a little bit of repositioning you can go ahead and have your helper draw your circle. One quarter of this circle will be used at the corner itself.

5 FLUIDITY

Fluidity is a natural progression from accuracy. It is hard to show fluidity, if the horse lacks straightness and is unable to produce smooth accurate shapes. An incredible ice skater, ballet dancer, or musician who demonstrates fluidity in their movements, in their skills, and in their performance can only do so after years of training and honing their accuracy.

If fluidity is a natural progression from accuracy, then why do we need a chapter for it. The answer is that we can improve the look of fluidity by being aware of where the horse is and where the horse needs to move to. We can think of how the horses body must be positioned from one movement to the next, we can think of the changes of direction ahead of us and we can think in terms of how to smoothly move from one gait to the next.

This chapter will give you some hints and tips on how to improve your fluidity and show your horse to its best advantage. It will cover both movements and strategies for riding a better test.

Preparation

One must always be thinking one movement ahead and the most basic improvement you can make is to make a slight bend before you begin your turns. Even when going large you should have a very slight bend to the inside and just before moving off on your circle, perhaps a few strides before, you should generate the bend suitable for the circle or turn you are about to make.

As an aside, you would often hear me in lessons say that preparation is for the unprepared. What I mean by this, is that I disapprove of the general shortening of reins, taking more contact, doing obligatory half halts or any of the traditional fuss which is often associated with preparation. That is to say, if you were to do a downward transition, or an upward transition, your horse should be ready and already balanced for the transition. The kind of preparation I am talking about in this chapter is more strategic in nature, in the context of riding an entire test.

One of the most strategic ways of preparation is to know your horse and know the typical mistakes your horse makes. If your horse falls in, or falls out on turns then you should be aware of this. If your horse falls in then you need to make sure your inside leg and inside rein is ready and the opposite goes for horses that fall out. If your horse has a problem with quarters in during canter then you will know you will need to position your horse in shoulder-in. Do not be surprised by your horses known issues, you should manage them, you should be there and not be reactive. There is no excuse to be surprised when your horse does what he normally does, when he normally does it!

To give you a better idea of fluidity I am going to take part of an imaginary test, which is suitable for preliminary test levels and talk you through the movements as I would be thinking whilst doing the test.

Example 1

1.Enter the arena at A and proceed down the centre line.

My thinking on this changes depending whether I enter from within the arena or from the outside. I will talk about entering at A from inside the arena as this is the most difficult. Before I even entered this test, I will already be on the appropriate rein and diagonal in preparation for the turn at C.

I will also know how far away from the a marker I will begin my turn. If the bell rings and I am close to the A marker I will generally make another pass around the arena before coming up the centreline. The British dressage rulebook states that you have 45 seconds from the moment the bell rings to commence your test. 45 seconds is enough time to get around the arena again, so don't feel pressured. Just before I make my turn up the centre line I create a slight bend to the inside and then commence the turn at the known distance from the A marker. The moment I make the turn I look up at the C marker and keep my eyes fixed on it while making small adjustments as needed to get my horse onto the centre line.

Once on the centre line I keep the C marker between the horses ears and ride focused and forward to the marker.

2. At C turn right

To turn right at C I have to know exactly where I will be starting my turn, i.e. exactly how far away from the C marker I will begin turning my horse. More specifically I will need to know the radius of the quarter circle I'm using to make the turn. Just before I begin my turn I bend the horse to the right, look right and then begin the turn. I also know where on the track I should hit to the right of C and that is where I am looking as I begin the turn. As I approach the corner I must apply the same thinking as the turn at C. I must know the radius of the quarter circle I used to make the corner.

3. B circle right 20 m diameter

Just before reaching B I create a bend to the inside appropriate for the 20 m circle. The horse steps away from the track at B and I'm already looking across to the point crossing the centreline that I must step onto to be accurate. I continue this process to each quarter of the circle always thinking ahead one quarter. As I make my way back to B I know that I must go large so look up and down the long side and begin to straighten out my horse.

4. Between F & A Working Canter right

If the horse has trouble getting the correct lead for canter right it may be because it leans on the left shoulder, so as I approach the F marker I make sure that I have my outside aids on more clearly and that the horse is straight. Even as I give the aids for canter I still work on making sure the horse stays off its outside shoulder and is therefore more likely to strike off correctly to the right. If I were to simply go through the motions and create an inside bend for the corner and for the strike off, then it is likely I would restrict my horses inside shoulder, push it onto its outside shoulder and encourage it to strike off incorrectly.

Example 2

1. C working trot.

I am in walk, coming up to C on the right rein. I need to make sure that my walk is active, make a little bit of an extra effort to lift my horses back and just before the C marker give the aids to trot, working to make sure my horse stays up over its back through the transition. I have a slight bend to the inside and perform my usual quarter circle in the corner.

2. HXF 10 meter loop in from the track.

It is very easy to come out of the corner and begin your loop. I make sure I keep going to H, that I have an inside bend and that my horse steps off at H. I'm already looking at X and as I approach it I begin to change the horses bend, first straight then bend to the left. I am now looking just before F and as I approach F I straighten the horse then create a slight bend to the inside just as I step onto the track just before F.

7. A Medium Walk

As I come out of the corner – I straighten my horse up for the transition to walk. Although I recommend maintaining a slight inside bend when travelling around the arena I prefer to be straight during transitions, so I straighten the horse up and make the transition to walk asking slightly before the marker.

From the above examples I hope you can notice that a lot of my focus is on the transitions between movements. On the change of bend from one direction to the other, on the readiness of my horse to make a transition from one pace to another and the element of thinking ahead always to the next movement or part of movement.

By focusing on fluidity and that part of fluidity which is preparation you will help your horse to maintain balance, you will create an air of competence and improve the harmony between you and your horse.

Riding a fluid test needs a strategic thinking rider who has put thought into the test before they even perform it. At home I like to practice my tests in sections, so for example I will practice turning up the centreline and turning right or turning left. This allows me to practice connections between movements without the horse starting to anticipate. You will of course be mixing the sections of the test up into different orders and sometimes even reversing the movements. The main point is to learn how to fluidly fit together the elements of your test.

What to do when the movement is lacking fluidity?

Let's take the movement of two half 10m circles from E to B in working Trot. The section in which most people have difficulty in fluidity is the change of bend through X and horses lose their fluidity in a number of ways. They can be stiff to change bend, they can lose their energy through X, they can fall out or fall in and sometimes they can hollow.

In most of the above issues, the judge will merely write 'lacking suppleness'. In general I will always make sure that my horse can trot a 10m circle with balance and a good rhythm before I decide to do to two half 10m meter circles. The reason for this is that I need to be sure that my horse is supple in both directions for this size of circle, before I have any hope of asking him to change bend in the middle of one of the circles.

Once you've got to the stage of having your horse supple on a 10 m circle, but you find it's still difficult to do the two half 10m meter circles, specifically the change of bend in the centre, then you should try the following (see diagram below); simply trot over X straight for a few more strides, smoothly change the bend and then continue on the half circle.

Practice this variation of the two half 10m circles until it becomes more fluid, then the next step is to simply reduce the period of time spent on the centre line. If you have taken my advice of always having a very slight inside bend even when going large and preparing your horse for any turn with a slight prebend then this movement, when presented to the horse in its natural progression of training, will not present much of a problem.

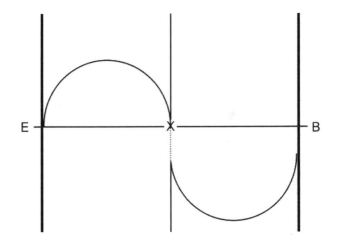

Diagram 16 – Training the change of bend.

Fluid Transitions

I will always prefer fluidity and smoothness over expediency when training the horse. This applies to movements as well as transitions. When I wish to train a horse to move from walk to trot, round over its back and smooth, I will allow it to take as many number of steps as is required to achieve this. I prefer this to blasting the horse from walk to trot regardless of his outline.

Remember the horse must understand how to move his body in the manner you want through the transition and he does not do this by coming to some intellectual realisation, but more so through trial, error and reward from the rider. The rider's job is to make sure that their biomechanics are set up in such a way as to make the outcome that they want be the most likely one.

Fluidity Tactics Summary

- Prepare your horse for a turn or circle with a slight prebend.
- Know ahead of time the radius of the circle that is appropriate for the turns you need to make.
- Prefer smoothness over expediency when training your horse. You only get better at what you practice, so to practice a hollow transition is to get better at being hollow in transitions. I would prefer a slower transition but done smoothly as this teaches the horse the correct biomechanics for the transition. The transition will become more instant over time as the horse ingrains the biomechanics in his neurology.
- Practice sections of your test and focus on the transition from one movement to the next.
- List out your horses known difficulties and write down how they affect the movements in your test. How would you ride to combat these?
- If you are having difficulty with the movement or combination of movements, how can you break these down into simple to perform movements and then gradually increase the difficulty to the required level.
- Always make sure that you have the appropriate bend for the turn or circle you are performing. I often see riders bend too much to the inside, even on 20m circles, thus making their life more difficult if they need to change the bend.

The joy of a fluid horse which is ready to respond when you want is hard to describe. However, I am reminded of a time, when I used to work in a riding school as an instructor and working pupil. I used to ride a train a particular mare more than the other school horses, because she initially needed it and then because I liked riding her. It was about that time when I had actually made a breakthrough in understanding how to turn smoothly.

This mare and I got on so well, that I could be in sitting trot and just turn almost by thinking it. We could do 4 or 5 loop serpentines and turn at will in any direction. I often used her for demonstrations, which I did once in a while, because even way back then I was trying to write descriptions for pupils on paper of how to improve.

To be able to work on fluidity, one must first be able to focus, to keep one's mind in the present and relating that to upcoming short-term events. It is essentially planning on how we get from where we are to where we want to be as smoothly as possible. A rider who is away with the fairies, worrying about what people might be thinking of their test, or perhaps worrying about their last mistake will not be able to plan, think about the next movements and will therefore lose fluidity and appear to be surprised when their horse makes the same mistake it always makes in the same place.

In the chapter on practice I talk about ways to improve your concentration, to improve your focus and to cut down the chatter in your mind. I believe I have a very high level of focus, in fact at one time I was asked if I liked riding by someone who watched me school a horse. I had to reply that I loved riding however the look on my face was my "concentrated face" and that I could do nothing about it! It only ever improves when I have brain space enough to both ride and put a smile on my face!

Peter Dove

A CLASSICAL VIEW ON FLUIDITY

by Demelza Hawes

For me, being both classical and competitive, my passion is truly the horse's movement and working with what nature has given him, developing it and encouraging his expression within it.

From breaking in, to advanced competition and training, it is vital that the horse is comfortable in his movement, confident and desiring to show himself off. Not in an overtly precocious manner, but with pride, nobility and fluidity.

The word fluidity can mean many things to many people. I consider it a certain smoothness, acceptance and desire to move with agility, grace and puissance. We, as riders, need not hinder this natural given mobility. When a horse is young or in his early education, it is imperative to follow the horse in his natural swing, gradually allowing him to accept our leg aids and come into a very elastic, forgiving contact which never fixes or constrains. As a horse then develops, reactions become quicker, more astute from the leg and seat and the contact becomes more directional and useable. The key is to keep this fluid movement within this framework.

Classical training is very much based upon exercises, which play an important role developing balance, suppleness, rhythm and then collection. The use of transitions, from pace to pace and within paces are also paramount, whilst maintaining and searching for smoothness and fluidity.

Each different exercise, from the humble but incredibly valuable 20metre circle, to the shoulder-in need to be ridden with smoothness and balance. Riding each step, positioning and allowing the horse to fulfil the right sequence and placement of steps is very important. So, when riding and training a specific exercise, fluidity and regularity of steps is a vital focus point, all balanced by the magic half halt. Once each exercise or pattern begins to feel easy then the progression naturally leads you to the next.

The key, therefore, to good training and development is the progression from one exercise to the next. Preparation and achievement then feeds into the next stage.

This emphasis on fluid movement also relates to your warm-up. When training and at competition, the process of making your horse ready for the test (or if training, then the next difficulty of exercise), is a progressive affair. One starts with simple movements which gradually increase in difficulty and demand, one exercise feeding into the next, fluidly.

Having trained in France with the Cadre Noir (home of so many Masters through history), the use of exercises, especially lateral, became our staple diet, in all disciplines. The importance of progression from exercise to exercise, and the balance within those is what contributes to advancing the horse and leading them to high school movements. Used by the Masters they are very much still relevant today and their theories are in sync with the horse's biomechanics. Great focus, feel and discipline as well as patience are all attributes which need mastering to really achieve a good fluidity of training and fluidity in the movements.

Each time we sit on or work with our horses we are training them and influencing them. Be sure that it's a positive experience and you will go far. All the elements within this book aim to give guidance and support so you can achieve your goals and create a happy, agile horse...what could be better!!!? We all love to move easily, so encourage and enable your horse to so the same.

Demelza Hawes

International Classical Dressage Rider/Trainer and Partner of Nicolas Bordas, French Eventer and FEI level III trainer.

http://www.hawesbordas.com

Peter Dove

6 UNDERSTANDING

The phrase understanding can seem rather nebulous, but we shall break it down into its component parts during this chapter. There are many things we need to understand to be successful at dressage. We need to understand the purpose of school movements, the purpose of dressage tests, how to select the next steps in our training and understand typical issues and corrections. It's also really important to understand what judges are looking for and what the typical comments really mean. Finally it's really important to understand what it is that we do not understand! What are the signs in our riding, training and results that should flag to us that we lack understanding in some key area.

The purpose of school movements and exercises

Rather than list every possible school movement or exercise we can break them down into circles, transitions, lengthening of strides, shortening of strides, stretching exercises and lateral work. I do not intend in this chapter to cover every element, but to give you a basic idea of what benefit you can derive from these exercises.

Circles will help improve the horses balance, rhythm, suppleness, straightness and strength of hind legs. Straightness may seem to be a strange one to include, however the mere task of remaining balanced through both shoulders and not falling in or out on the circle will improve the horse straightness. The inside hind leg has to step a little underneath the body and therefore has to work a little harder. This will help develop strength and surety of footing.

Transitions both upwards and downwards teach the horse to engage its quarters. In the upward transitions the horse must push from behind and in downward transitions the horse must engage the hindquarters and use the hind legs to assist braking. The transitions also teach the horse to listen to the rider and can often be used as a tool to rebalance the horse.

Lengthening and shortening of strides teaches the horse different ways of loading and using its hind legs, as well as ingraining tempo and rhythm and developing strength in the hindquarters. The horse learns to move its centre of gravity forwards and backwards and still maintain balance. It improves the flexibility of the hocks and the horses general elasticity.

Stretching, as in free walk on a long rein and stretching in trot, improves the horses top line, confirms the horses reach into the rein and is almost the equivalent of touching your toes! This teaches the horse to trust the hand, to reach towards it and to develop a frame which can be both shortened and lengthened without resistance. It is a great suppling exercise.

Lateral work ushers in a new era of suppleness, flexibility and power. Shoulder-in strengthens the horse's hind legs because of the amount that the inside hind leg must step underneath the body. It also teaches the horse to be able to position its shoulders at the rider's request.

On Bend

In the spirit of understanding I thought I would just go a little bit more into bend and what it should look like.

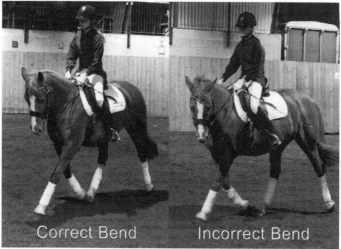

Correct Bend   **Incorrect Bend**

Photo 6

In general riders tend to 'bend' their horses too much, especially riders who have been around more and know that they should show an inside bend. Less experienced riders often suffer from not showing enough bend, or perhaps outside bend on circles and turns. Many people take up the phrase 'more bend', perhaps from a dressage sheet and incorrectly interpret it.

In Photo 6 my daughter demonstrates the difference on her mare Soley Magick Tinkerbell. The version on the left has correct bend for a 20m circle and shows even balance through the shoulders. The second version is the most common form of bend I see, where the inside shoulder is somewhat restricted and the horse is pushed onto its outside shoulder. Look at the difference between the two, have a look at how even and balanced the horse is on the left. Notice the lines of energy in the first photo that travel true from behind into a forward movement, whereas in the second photo they are dissipating out through the outside shoulder.

Milly of course shows a couple of faults of her own in both photos such as her lower leg is a little too far back, though this is exaggerated by the viewing angle and I would prefer her hands a little more carried. Some of the more hawk eyed of you may also notice that the first photo is closer to E.

This type of incorrect bend comes from thinking of steering the horse through the nose. Mary Wanless calls the 2nd version 'jack-knifing' like when a lorry jack-knifes, the nose is pointing left, but the rest of the shoulder is going right. More extreme versions of jack-knife I call 'turning left and stepping right', or 'turning right and stepping left'. This is where the horse seems to be pointed in one direction but all the legs are pedaling in opposite direction.

This subtle mistake can happen all the way up the levels in dressage and I have seen even advanced horses and riders making this basic error. When we drop balance in favour of bend, to perform a circle smaller than the horse is ready for, is when this error shows itself. Stated slightly differently, I believe this is because we are seduced by the supposed suppleness we are generating. It's very easy to feel when a horse falls in, but falling out seems to catch us out more easily.

Suppleness is not so much about how well we can bend our horse to the inside, but more about does the horse easily maintain balance and appropriate bend for the shapes it is performing. Can the horse change its bend smoothly and easily without losing balance, becoming tense or stiff and changing tempo?

I already gave the you the visualisation of riding on top of a balance beam which should help. It can help to think of steering the horse more from the withers than from the nose. It is also important to realise, contrary to a lot of teachings, that we turn our horse from our outside aids, not our inside aids. It is often said that you should have the horse bent around your inside leg, which is why I think riders focus so much on the inside aids. Thinking too much of the 'bend around the inside leg' is a quick way to pushing your horse onto its outside shoulder. Yes it should feel like the horse is bent around the inside leg, but this shouldn't be because of lots of dominant inside leg action!

A horse will move away from any given stimulus, meaning that if I were to push him from the left, he will move to the right. If we want our horse to turn right, we have to provide a force from the left to do so, thus we use our outside aids when turning. Think about that for a moment and I am sure you will realise why inside leg and hand will doom you to falling out.

Finally, one other consequence of using the inside rein and pushing with the inside leg, is that you will end up restricting and tying in the inside shoulder. The horse will begin to become more stiff and less expressive through its shoulders in the way its steps onto turns and circles. I hope you can see that much just from the two photographs.

You can use this idea of 'stimulus' to solve both falling in and falling out. If the horse is falling in, we need to push him back out using the inside aids. This is actually pretty intuitive for most riders, though some do get trapped into pulling on the outside rein. In falling in, our inside rein and inside leg, push the shoulder back into its proper place.

The purpose of this book is not to teach the biomechanics of riding and for more detailed information on turning, steering, straightness, and other techniques I would direct you to my own coach Mary Wanless, who's books do an incredible job of teaching rider biomechanics.

Medium Walk

Photo 7

In medium walk the horse should be active, show over-track and good ground cover. The walk should also remain relaxed and fluid with a steady and clear four beat. Though its hard to tell in the photo, Milly would only get a 7 as she would need to march on a little more.

Some of the things that would lose marks for you in walk would be tempo too slow or too fast, lacking energy, horse not over-tracking (not enough ground cover), inconsistent outline, unsteady to contact, outside bend, too much inside bend and falling on shoulder, inaccuracy, too short in the neck, overbent , hollowing, 4 beat not clear, pacing and jogging.

Just to be clear, over-tracking occurs when the horses hind leg hoof steps in front of the hoof print left by the foreleg. How much over-track occurs is down to several factors and really depends on the capability of your horse. Over-track is a symptom of a correct, relaxed and active walk. Then the question of how much depends on how much activity, stretch and relaxation the horse has and its conformation.

Free Walk On A Long Rein (British Dressage) - Stretching on a Long Rein (FEI)

There are a number of pre-requisites to getting a horse to do a good free walk on a long rein, some of them are ride pre-requisites and some are horse pre-requisites.

One of the requirements is 'long rein', which is specified to avoid the 'loose rein'. There should not be loops in the rein, and furthermore the requirement shows that your horse can follow the contact and is happy to do so. Free walk on a long rein, and moving back to medium, is a good training step for teaching the horse to lengthen and shorten its frame, with no tension, reading it for collected and medium/extended paces.

The main mistake riders make when teaching this to the horse is that they throw the reins at the horse in varying degrees hoping the horse will stretch. Let me say that you have to be an awful lot sneakier than that! Here is a little exercise for you to try right now.

Put your hands in front of you as if you are holding the reins. Now try to imagine there is a slight weight there of the contact the horse is maintaining with you. Next try to push your hands forward, but do this so smoothly and so slowly that someone watching would barely notice it happening. This skill is a must, this is the opposite of giving the reins to have a loop happen. Its very important not to just let the reins slip and have no control of the length of the frame of the horse. This lack of control over the length of the frame may lead to snatching of the reins and an inconsistent stretch. You must have course allow the reins to lengthen, but it should be done under your control.

Another tip that I can offer it to lighten your seat slightly as you offer the reins, by tipping forward slightly and taking more weight into your thighs. This shouldn't be necessary once the horse has the idea but it's a good hint to the horse that you would like him to stretch over his back.

If you start your schooling session and your horse won't stretch then its worth trying it a little later when he is a more tired and wanting to stretch. Then with your combination of giving hands and light seat, he will start to get the idea. Suffice to say the horse must be paying attention to the rider and be relaxed. If the horse is away with the fairies, he will be far too 'up periscope' to want to stretch. The rider to must have a still seat, and not be shoving the saddle into the horses back.

Working Trot

Photo 8

What should an intro/prelim/training horse look like? We all try so very hard to ride well and get our horse looking correct. Should you find your horse tense, cramped, going overbent and becoming short in the neck, it may be that you are expecting too much at the level you are at.

Photo 8 is an intro level pony, soon to be moving to prelim/training level. Its always difficult showing a work in progress but I hope this photo gives the general idea of correct work at this level.

Criticisms about this photo are that I would like to see a little more energy and muscle tone in the horse.

Praise for the photo, the mare is going reasonably forward (though a tiny bit off tracking up), freely. The neck comes nicely out of the shoulders upwards, ending up with the nose being vertical and a nice space where the gullet is. Milly is doing a good job keeping her hands forward in front of her. You will also notice that if we were to take the horse out from underneath her, she would land in balance on the arena floor.

She is doing rising/posting trot and is half way from the top of the rise to the bottom.

This is the kind of outline you should be looking for at this level. If this were consistently maintained around the arena on an accurate circle I would give it an 8 with the comment, "needs a little more energy".

Tracking up should happen in working trot. Tracking up means that the horse's hind leg hoof lands in the hoof print left behind by the foreleg on the same side. Tracking up is a good sign of activity, freedom and relaxation of movement.

Typical problems, which will lose marks in working trot, are: not tracking up, lacking energy, unsteady to contact, hollow, falling in/out, head tilting, tempo too quick, running, tight or short in the neck, overbent, flat trot(not enough jump between diagonal pairs), inaccuracy in movement, not enough reach into the rein or stretch on movements that require it, walking and so on into the range of behaviour deemed as disobedience (bucking, spinning etc).

Transition into canter

Getting a horse to strike off on the correct lead is a typical problem for many riders and they are inadvertently making it difficult for the horse to achieve it. We are often told that to prepare for canter we should create a bend to the inside and then ask. For a horse that has problems getting the correct lead on a specific rein, or isn't balanced through its shoulders, this advice can be misplaced especially if the rider proceeds to emphasise the bend believing it will somehow increase the chance the horse will go off on the correct lead.

Lets look at why the horse would choose to lead with the correct leg. On the right rein the horse will generally choose to lead with the right foreleg. This is because the horse will then have the widest base to the inside and therefore the most stability. Now lets imagine, you are on the right rein, you decide to create a bend to the inside causing your horse to fall onto his left shoulder. You are now making it more likely he will lead onto the wrong leg, because as far as he is concerned he is actually leaning to the left and onto his left shoulder. When you create too much bend to the inside, you could be accidentally restricting his inside foreleg and making it far less likely he will lead with it.

I think everyone knows that it is easier to ask a horse to canter in the corner, as this is meant to give the horse the best chance to go onto the correct lead. But the reason you should ask in the corner, is because your horse should be inclined to lead with his inside foreleg providing the wide base to the inside to support himself around the turn. So as I ask for canter, on a young horse, I make sure the shoulders are coming around the corner slightly to the inside. In really difficult cases, where the horse won't take the correct lead, you can keep a small amount of outside bend to really emphasise pushing the shoulders to the inside. Naturally as the horse learns to match the aids to the correct lead and he develops better balance, your bend can return to normal.

Everyone should know the sequence of the canter legs. The sequence begins outside hind, then the inside hind and outside fore land as a diagonal pair, then finally the inside fore leg. The horse then pulls/pushes itself off the ground in a jump and the sequence begins again. Try to see a slow motion video of canter and you will see it more clearly.

Now we have sequence in mind I will explain the aids I give to ask a horse to canter. We are speaking of an inexperienced horse when I talk about these aids. I will always ask the horse in the corner, I make sure that the horse is even through both shoulders going into the corner. I will go into sitting trot. As I go into sitting trot I will press inwards with my inside leg, as a kind of precursor to the transition, a form of 'get ready' to the horse. Then my outside leg will go back and deliver a little kick which will rebound back off the horses side – meaning I do not keep the aid on. My seat will have my outside seat bone back and I keep the hands still. The time difference between the inside leg and the outside leg is just a small pause, maybe a second long. Count it like, "One.. and two". 'One' is the inside leg, 'two' is the outside leg.

So in brief those are the aids I use, now to the why of it. The reason I will use my outside leg in a little kick like this is to shock the outside hind leg underneath the body to start the sequence of canter off. After the initial training of the horse to the strike off, you can ease off the strength of the aid and just use a light touch with the leg. Fast forward many years of training and you will see horses doing one time flying changes with the riders delivering alternate leg back aids. I hope this helps you. As a final tip, if the horse does not 'jump' away from the leg into canter, you may have to carry the whip in the outside hand and give him a little tap as you apply your outside leg.

Typical Rider Mistakes

I see a lot of mistakes at the lower levels and even more persistent mistakes into the higher levels from riders. In this small section I want to increase your understanding by talking about some of the typical mistakes in position and application of aids when schooling a horse. There are a lot more than I can list here, I just want to cover the most obvious ones as I see it.

Shoving with the seat

The rider has probably heard that they must go with the horses movement, be supple or perhaps that they must drive the horse forward with their seat. I often see riders attempting to encourage their horses forward by using their seat. Let's take a step back and have a look at the likely consequence of doing this.

As we push our seat in the saddle, this is likely to increase the pressure downwards and forwards onto the saddle and therefore into the horses back. The horse will hollow its back and attempt to rush forwards and away from the uncomfortable pressure it finds there. In effect the rider has achieved the desired outcome of the horse speeding up. However other much less desirable outcomes occur. The horse hollows his back away from the riders seat, he lifts his head and neck up away from the riders contact, lengthens his underneath and speeds up by going faster with his forehand doing all the work.

The terms 'using the seat' or 'driving with the seat' are the most misunderstood, but most used terms in dressage. They mean many things to different people and the vast majority of interpretations are erroneous. The riders seat should be still, as if the rider grows out of the top of the horse like a carousel pole. The is no shoving or pushing and the rider remains molded to the horses back.

I often ask my pupils a trick question "Who is

responsible for keeping the horse going forwards". Inevitably they say "I am responsible". However the truth is the exact opposite. It is the horse's responsibility to keep doing what you last told it to do. If you ask your horse to move forwards, it should keep doing so without constant reminding. The leg asks the horse to move forwards, not the seat, the seat allows this to happen.

You may then be asking how are you supposed to use your seat. The simple answer is "You are not", the complex answer would take another book to investigate! At this stage you are doing your horse the biggest favour by being still.

Using too much hand

We all want our horses to show that beautiful dressage outline of the horse 'on the bit' or as Mary Wanless calls it 'The Seeking Reflexes'. This is the feeling that the horse reaches out towards the rider's hand to a steady contact, the back lifts and the horse's sides fill out. The horse feels half a hand higher. Getting the horse to work in an outline is a huge topic which cannot be covered in this book. I would suggest you have a look at the 'On the bit webinar series' advert at the end of the book.

I will say the following; if you find yourself fiddling with the reins, obsessed with getting your horses head down, fighting with the contact or other issue of contact then get yourself a good rider biomechanics coach. Let me say that once you know how to lift a horses back, get it to reach into the rein and seek the contact, getting a horse to work in an outline is easy. Until you get there it can seem a difficult task. Do not get seduced into thinking getting the horses head down is what dressage is about.

This is probably a good place to mention BTV. No it's not some terrible horse disease but an often used acronym for Behind The Vertical. When a horse is correctly 'on the bit' the nose should be on the vertical or slightly in front of the vertical. A horse behind the vertical could be a sign that the rider is using excessive force to position the horse's head, or that the horse is so afraid of the bit that it keeps its head tucked in away from the contact.

Before we give BTV a black mark and brand all riders who have their horse BTV bad riders it is important to realise that this can happen normally in the course of training, and of course there are degrees of the problem. It ranges from the hideous and banned Rollkur to a slightly amount behind the vertical. Personally I think a lot of the correctly righteous ire against Rollkur gave any kind of BTV a bad name.

Behind the vertical will always happen at some point with all riders. The horse is carrying a heavy weight (its head) on the end of a long neck. Sometimes it will drop it too low if its tired, so even amongst the best and most ethical riders you will no doubt be able to catch this happening unless they play it way too safe and trot around hollow. As a judge I always penalise BTV but it must be taken into context with other elements of the test. After all the test is not just about whether the horse can remain on or in front of the vertical throughout the entirety of the test. It does become a problem if BTV is a consistent feature.

Some of the ways in which the horse can be seen BTV are the following:

- Horse was previously trained that way and rider is attempting to fix.
- Horse is young, or tired and has dropped BTV.
- Horse has fallen onto its forehand and is leaning on the rider's hand.
- The horse's topline has become too long in relation to its underline.

There are of course many bad reasons why the horse may be BTV but I really don't want to discuss these things, suffice to say we want to train our horses to be on, or slightly infront of the vertical, and if your horse is BTV you should know why and be attempting to correct it.

Photo 9 is a montage showing different head positions with a comment. These are photos of Tinker.

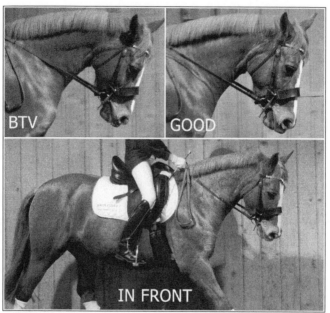

Photo 9

The element of the photo labeled BTV was a moment when Tinker became a little tired and went onto the forehand, leaning into the rider's hand. This would be the most BTV I would expect to see.

The element of the photo labeled GOOD is almost right and some may argue needs to be a touch more infront. Finally the element of the photo labeled IN FRONT shows the horse very slightly infront of the vertical. It's a little harder to see as the last photo is not quite at 90 degrees onto the horse, but it was in front.

I hope this section has thrown some light onto BTV, and hopefully will allow you to correctly spot it. In summary, a small element of BTV will happen from time to time for a variety of reasons, but it should not be a consistent or severe feature of your horse's way of going.

Reducing power to maintain control

Another issue I see is the rider, in an attempt to keep their horse round, will reduce the power of the horse so that he does not hollow so much. Most judges will penalise the rider for this and I can only refer you to my previous section on overuse of hand. This is often done in combination with sitting trot. It is always very jarring to see sitting trot at the lower levels, especially at intro/prelim/training level. The horse is usually not ready to carry the rider in sitting trot. It has not developed the strength in his back and the stability in his outline. If you find it difficult to control your horse's tempo and find yourself having to drastically reduce power then have a look at the rider biomechanics section at the back of the book which gives advice on improving rider stability, balance, and tempo control through correct rider biomechanics. Riding well and doing the best for our horses, is hard and requires us to be honest, strive to improve, and be on the same team as the horse, despite how difficult things may seem to be.

Leaning in direction of bend.

This happens more so at the lower levels on turns and circles, but often makes its appearance again as riders start to do lateral work. Here the use of mirrors will help you greatly. Collapsing or leaning off to one side will make it harder for you and your horse to stay straight and level through his shoulders. You should always attempt to keep your chin over the mane (over the centre line of the horse). Check yourself out next time you make a turn, circle or some lateral work, can you keep your spine 90 degrees to the horses spine?

This kind of mistake is often due to a misunderstanding of so called 'weight aids'. I really have very little time for such descriptions because 99% of the time they are interpreted incorrectly and also because they do not have to mentioned at all in correct teaching. Weight aids happen as a consequence of a correctly positioned body. If anyone mentions weight aids to you, get them to be very specific in their descriptions of what you have to do. If it involves, leaning, or weighting seat bones, or collapsing etc. then stay away from it – the torso should always remain stacked over the pelvis.

Lower leg moving in rising/posting trot (over use of leg)

If you find that your lower leg moves forwards and backwards as you do rising trot, then it may be that you are either using your legs too much or that your rising trot mechanism isn't correct.

If it's because you are using your leg each time you sit, then you need to rethink how you are training your horse to go from your leg aids. Each time you use your leg, you should get a result. The horse should move more forwards than he was doing before. If you use your leg simply to keep the horse going, you are training him to ignore your leg since you are essentially saying "My leg means do nothing different".

I generally find it is easy to teach a person, on a lazy horse, to train the horse to be more sensitive. Firstly you have to become extremely responsible about how you use your leg. As the coach, I often say to the rider, that they can only use their leg when I say 'leg'. Upon using the leg, the rider must expect the horse to move forwards. If there is no response to the leg aid, the rider will need to repeat the aid and at the same time give the horse a tap with the whip. This should be enough to make the horse step forwards. The rider of course should be expecting this and be sat securely in place and allow the horse to move more forwards. Then we go back to being still with the leg. In this way we can teach the horse that leg means go with more energy. Gradually you will teach him that he should be going willingly forwards as a default state. We should not have to nag and kick just to have him stay in trot. Remember the responsibility of the horse is to keep doing what you last told him to do and its your responsibility to make it the easiest thing for him to comply.

If your lower leg is moving of its own accord and you can't keep it still no matter how hard you try then help is at hand. Firstly be comforted by the fact that a lot of people have this problem, its not just you. Its also NOT a sign that you are somehow inept. Its just that you don't know how yet. Once you have the right how you will get it. Mary Wanless has an excellent video on tempo control which talks about the rising trot mechanism and how it should work. At the end of the book I have a resources section for such helpful videos. In essence it boils down to whether you are kneeling up and down to do rising trot, or standing up and down by pushing off your foot.

If you push off your foot to do rising trot, you will not be able help moving your lower leg. It helps to think of the knee as the pivot point and kneeling up and down, with no weight changing in the foot and the lower leg being still. Watch the video from the resources section, well worth the investment of time!

Photo 10

To understand the mechanics of rising trot we should ask ourselves the question, why do we do rising trot? On the sit and on the top of rise the horse has a single diagonal pair on the ground as in photo 10. He jumps between the diagonal pairs, and we are either going up, or going down for the duration of the jump. Now imagine that we do a small rise... what could be consequence of that? Firstly it restricts the height the horse is encouraged to jump and therefore the length of the stride, secondly it always means we are behind the movement and not matching the forces generated by the horse.

In rising trot the lower leg should stay still and the pelvis describe the arc of circle with a still knee as the centre point. My ability to create impulsion, cadence and tracking up increased dramatically the day my teacher Mary Wanless described this to me all those years ago.

You can see that in photo 10 Milly has got to the top of the rise, but one thing to point out, is that she got there smoothly matching the forces generated by the horse. It is possible to over-thrust and be doing more than the horse is giving, but generally I see riders under-thrusting and keeping their horse underpowered. Milly is also a little hollow in her back, which isn't ideal meaning she has lengthened her front on the way up. The length of the front and the length of the back should remain the same.

There has been a tendency to want to make a smaller rise to slow the horse down if it is too fast, however we end up with small quick steps. It is better to slow the speed with which you go from the bottom of the rise to the top, and from the top of the rise to the bottom. Watch Mary's video explanation – its very useful.

The purpose of tests

When you are riding a dressage test you are not just doing a test, you are demonstrating the current state of your horses training. And to some people that mere thought alone, helps reduce nervousness. After all this is not an exam we are taking, in which you will fail or pass. Each of the movements within the test demonstrates something to the judge and it is up to you to understand what it is that you are demonstrating.

My purpose when writing this book, was not to list every movement and write up its purpose in some tabular format but rather to teach you to think more deeply about every movement you perform. So that you are never surprised by the marks or the comments given by the judge, because, after all, you already knew the current state of your horses training. A little later in this chapter I will talk about the skills of training, typical errors, the judges directives and expand on typical comments made by the judge.

Selecting next steps

Another important reason for understanding all of the school movements and exercises you can perform and the effect on the horse and its training is so that you can select the next best step for the horse to take. Imagine you are training a young horse and all you have been doing so far is 20m circles. How would you know when you are ready to do a 15m circle, or begin three loop serpentine's, or half 10m circles. How would you know when your horses ready to go from trot to halt after only doing trot to walk.

I remember schooling a friend's horse a long while back and being asked when finishing a 20m circle why I looked so happy. To me the horse had been straight, rhythmical, consistent in its outline and to the contact, had good energy and the circle was extremely accurate. My thought had been at that point was "I think we're ready to move on to 15m circles!". I choose to do more difficult movements based on how well the horse fulfils basic requirements of the less difficult movement. It isn't based upon whether I'm bored of doing 20m circles, or whether "we really ought to be doing 15m circles by now", or even by any artificially set goals such as competition dates.

Now to be fair I had already started a few 15m circles with that horse, because he had reached a sufficiently good standard at 20m circles. I just didn't want to leave you with the impression that I wait for perfection before moving on to a more difficult exercise.

Another good measure of when your horse is ready to move to a more difficult exercise is to simply try it; your horse will tell you if he is ready or not. If you encounter a lot of hardship and struggle, whilst trying the new movement then you are probably going too quickly. For instance, at a very basic level, moving from a 20m circle performed well to a 15m circle is not that big a deal, as the horse may find it a little harder to get round and may lose a little impulsion but all of these things should be easily managed by the rider.

I often get asked by riders when they should start teaching a horse to do lengthened strides and medium trot. My answer, a little flippantly, is "when the horse is ready for it". In my defence I always go on to explain in more detail. I can only tell you how it works for me, others may have different methods. The ability to do medium trot and lengthened horse strides comes at the stage where the horse begins developing impulsion. I know I am getting close to attempting medium trot or lengthened strides when I begin to feel the horse developing energy and that I could easily call on that energy. For instance I will begin to feel a cadence in the trot where the horse is maintaining a consistent tempo and feels as though if I would ask for more energy it would just happen in balance. At that point I would attempt lengthened strides, and more often than not we get a few nice strides immediately. As I said in a very simple example of the 15m circle, when trying something new it shouldn't be a strain, struggle or a fight to achieve it. It should progress naturally from the horse's current level.

When should we start lateral work? I will start lateral work when my horse is supple through a variety of different sized turns and circles, when I can place his shoulders easily onto and off turns and when I have good control of tempo. At this point my horse understands my leg to mean more than simply go faster, he understands it to mean bend more or to increase impulsion. I will start with demi pirouettes in walk, partly because my horse understands positioning his shoulders but also partly because it is a movement I find easy to train.

Demi-pirouette in walk is where the forehand walks a circle around the hind-legs which are doing a smaller semi circle. It is also called 'turn on the haunches'. The more advanced horses keep their inside hind-leg marching almost on the same spot making a very small half circle, with the body pivoting around it. Don't get the impression from the word 'pivot' that the horse spins on that leg! The horse must keep the sequence of walk true and step with that inside hind leg. The horse should be slightly bent in the direction the turn is being executed. For younger horses, the hind-legs make a larger circle since they wont be strong enough to do a small one.

To execute demi-pirouette I will choose the markers A,E,B or C to perform the movement. Let's say we are on the left rein approaching B. As you approach the marker begin to slow down the walk by slowing your seat bones. You should already have a small inside bend, increase it very slightly, then using your outside aids (leg and hand), begin to push the horses forehand to the left all the while focusing on keeping the tempo under your control and maintaining the slight inside bend. Your plan is to keep turning 180 degrees. Keep the walk moving forwards, do not try for too small a circle with the hind legs and expect to come off the track a way. When I first try this exercise with a horse, I am delighted if I can feel the shoulders moving over and that we keep on walking without too much tension. Do expect the walk to slow down, your horse is now expending energy moving sideways, but we do not want it to grind to a halt or become tense. Make sure that you remain inside seat bone in advanced and outside seat bone back, that you remain with your chin over the mane and you do not twist your torso out of shape attempting to push the horse round.

Turn on the forehand is also a very good exercise in teaching the horse to move itself away from your leg. It helps loosen the horse behind the saddle and is another important introduction to lateral work.

When thinking about transitions I find it very easy to know when to start doing more difficult versions, such as trot to halt or walk to canter. For upward transitions I need my horse to already remain round through his transitions from walk to trot or trot to canter and be clearly off my leg. For downward transitions the horse needs to be performing its downward transitions from canter to trot and trot to walk smoothly and without pitching onto the forehand. It's easy to know when to try trot to halt, because the trot to walk seems to be so easy.

The scales of training

The scales of training are based on the German training system and have been adopted by British dressage among other institutions. The five elements of the training system are often depicted as a pyramid with the lowest level being the base for all of the others, see the diagram below.

Rhythm is quite rightly at the base of the pyramid. Rhythm also includes tempo; a relaxed horse will produce an even rhythm in a consistent tempo. Rhythm refers to the sequence of the beats, walk being a four beat movement, trot being a two beat movement and canter being a three beat movement.

Losing marks for rhythm, would typically occur due to tension, where perhaps the walk rhythm can break down, or perhaps in canter when lacking energy the canter is no longer three beat.

Though the word rhythm is used, I believe it is extremely important to have a consistent tempo and to be in control of that tempo. This requires good riding skills and a biomechanically correct rising trot and sitting trot.

Without the ability to control the tempo you cannot begin to train the other levels. For instance to control a horse's straightness you need to use your legs. If you have no control over the tempo the horse will simply speed up and still not be straight and therefore suppleness will not develop. At the end of the book, in the resources section, there will be a link to a list of videos which cover some of the basic biomechanics needed for tempo control.

Lateral suppleness will develop through work on turns and circles, longitudinal suppleness will develop through stretching exercises and working in an outline in the seeking reflexes, where the horse reaches over his back, over his top line and to the contact.

Once the horse has developed suppleness and especially longitudinal suppleness then a good contact should be the norm. There should be an even weight in both hands and the rider should also get a sense that the horses back is lifted in contact with their seat and that the horse sides are in contact with the riders thighs. Mary Wanless, author of the Ride With Your Mind books, calls this the seeking reflexes. Where the horse seeks contact with a bit, it's back lifts seeking contact with the rider seat and the horse sides fill out to the riders thighs. The opposite of the seeking reflexes is where the horses head retracts away from the riders hand, the back hollows away from the rider seat and their side's clamp down away from the riders legs in tension.

Without rhythm and tempo control suppleness, steady contact and impulsion cannot occur. Impulsion is energy under a tempo without excess tension. The horse learns to generate more energy per step within the same tempo and it is usually at this point that I begin to feel my horses ready for lengthening of strides in trot.

Straightness is next on the list and to some this may appear strange. After all, from the moment we stepped foot on circles and working on straight lines we are attempting to have our horse straight. The reason it comes after impulsion is that it is assumed that the horse will not be strong enough in its quarters to consistently and evenly place its feet where they need to be, so true and consistent straightness will not be there. I expect we have all experienced the slow and lazy horse meandering left and right as we attempt to keep it straight; it is easier to be straight with a little more impulsion!

Finally collection, the pinnacle of training, can only be achieved when all of the other steps are ingrained. You cannot have collection without a rhythm, with no suppleness, with an inconsistent contact, no impulsion and a lack of straightness! It is beyond the scope of this book to teach collection, however the horse will begin to lighten his forehand, engage its hind legs, lower the croup and take more weight on the hind legs which step closer to the centre of gravity. The horse will begin to look more uphill.

Knowing the scales of training will help keep you more honest and less likely to kid yourself that you are ready for more advanced work. Dressage judges use the scales of training to help them assess horses that appear in front of them during tests. Does the horse have a rhythm, is it in a consistent tempo, is it supple through its movements, is it consistent to the contact, does it have enough energy and so on.

The judges directives

The judges directives are what appears to the right of the mark on test sheets, at least those provided by British dressage. These are very useful reminders for the judge as to what they should be looking for in a particular movement. Let me give you some examples:

Change rein in medium trot. The directives for this movement could be quality of trot, regularity, tempo. Ground cover. Lengthening of frame.

Change rein in a free walk on a long rein. The directives for this movement could be regularity, purpose, stretching forwards and down, ground cover, suppleness of whole body.

Next time you get your sheet study these directives and if you have videoed your test apply them to yourself as if you were the judge. It may help you develop a greater understanding as to the requirements of the movement.

Judges comments

As judges that we are there to observe and make comments and not there to deliver lessons. Certainly in the time available and in the space available it's difficult to impart meaningful advice. In its place we restrict ourselves to comments which relate to the directives and the requirements of the movements.

It is difficult even for some of the more experienced riders to translate a judges comment into some actionable correction or changes to training they can make. With so few words written it is easy for the rider to misinterpret, especially if they are not aware of the scales of training and have an understanding of what the particular movements are demonstrating to the judge. Some typical comments are:

Needs more suppleness – this could mean you need to demonstrate more suppleness by improving your accuracy or fluidity. It could also mean that the horse is not yet supple enough for the movement being asked of it, perhaps the horse does not smoothly change bend, or perhaps does not show enough bend.

Inconsistent to contact – this could mean several things. It could mean that your horse does not maintain his head carriage steady, or that he is moving his head around playing with the contact, for instance a horse that flicks its head forward and back. Of all the different ways a horse could be inconsistent to the contact, they all mean one basic thing; that the horse has not yet learn to reach toward the contact over his back and over his neck in a consistent way.

Against hand – this normally occurs in downward transitions, but can be seen in upward transitions. It could mean the horse is throwing his head against the hand upwards, or that the horse is leaning against the riders hand.

Lacking/Losing Rhythm – this is used when referring to a

changing tempo, and also when the rhythm of the pace is breaking up. For instance if the walk becomes tense, or the horse begins anticipating canter. Some judges are more discerning and use the words tempo/rhythm more correctly.

Needs more jump – this is often used with the canter and means that the horse needs to make a bigger thrust off the ground each stride. Its usually a sign that the horse is rather flat in strides.

Going too deep, behind the vertical – the horse is behind the vertical either because he is too tight under the gullet (either through being behind the contact or horse/rider pulling) or because his head and neck are too low.

Needs to show more difference – often used in the medium paces to explain to the rider there needs to be more difference in the length of the strides between working and medium paces.

Needs more ground cover – this too is often used in the medium paces and in free walk to describe a lack of length of stride. Usually here the horse is not over tracking.

Tight over back – the horse is a little hollow or tense over back and does not reach correctly towards the contact.

Needs more energy, more impulsion – the horse needs to show more energy within an appropriate tempo.

Losing balance – this can happen in downward transition, changes of bend and so on, symptoms usually include tempo speeding up, loss of outline through hollowing or a even tripping.

Quarters in – usually in canter, the horse is swinging it's pelvis to the inside so that it is no longer straight.

Poor positioning – this is often used in lateral work to describe a poor preparation or beginning to a lateral movement. Another phrase to go with this would be 'losing positioning' which could mean the correct angle for the movement is varying or being lost.

On shoulders/On Forehand – horse is usually heavy in front, leaning on the rider's hand, with not enough impulsion and often losing its natural tempo in favour of speeding up. Sometimes too the horse will be on the forehand losing speed and energy.

Above bit, hollow – horse is lifting its head and hollowing it's back.

Tight/Short in neck – the horse's neck is too short – this can be due to tension, the horse drawing its head back away from the riders hand, or the rider pulling on the reins.

Needs to flow more freely forwards – the horse is probably being a little lazy to the rider's leg aids and needs to move more actively of its own accord. It can also mean the horse is holding tension through its body and therefore cannot step as freely and as actively as it should.

These comments are but just a few and I plan to add even more to the website as time goes by. When joining the weekly webinars you can always ask me if you come across a comment you don't understand, and I will do my best to interpret it.

When do we know we lack understanding?

It is very easy to get sucked into beating our heads against the proverbial brick wall. We get it beaten into our minds that if we were to simply try harder, things will improve. In my experience trying tends to look a lot different from doing, in fact trying tends to look an awful lot like failing in some cases!

To save you from my meandering explanations and additional verbiage I have simply made a list – hoorah!

1. You are unable to find a solution to an issue, or make headway within a couple of schooling sessions to a problem you and the horse are having.
2. You are not sure what you should be doing next in your schooling session.
3. The marks or comments you get in tests are out of sync with your expectations.
4. You hit a plateau in your improvement that you cannot seem to get past.
5. You find yourself making excuses as to why you and your horse cannot do x, y or z.

Naturally, with regards to item 5, there may be perfectly valid reasons why the horse or rider cannot achieve something, however I will say that the vast majority of sound, uncompromised horses are capable of a good level of dressage. Item 5 is a warning, to honestly evaluate and ask other professionals if your reasons are valid, before writing either yourself or your horse off.

7 PRACTICE

What is practice? Essentially, practice is anything that we are doing for the second time around onwards! This means that almost every time we do anything, we are training something either in ourselves or in our horses. What a responsibility that is! In training and riding everything matters, everything has a positive or negative effect on the situation.

I don't want this to cause paralysis by analysis where nothing happens because you have to spend forever assessing the implications, however I think pretty much everything we do, deserves some thought and care. It is very easy to fall into habits when riding, when training and even when handling our horses. It is the horse that ends up in trouble when it is confused by mixed signals and fuzzy training.

Schooling Practice

When schooling my horses, I always have a routine at the start that I follow. The reason for the same routine, is that I am giving myself a better chance, when in a strange place, of my horse following the routine and habit. Routine helps ingrain habits into the horse, habits that I want to stick. Practice is simply about ingraining good habits into the horse.

Whatever you decide to do when schooling, you need to make sure you have a high chance of success when attempting something new. Always stack the odds in your favour. When my horse is doing good 20m circles, I don't think 'right time for something harder' and start on 10m circles. I make my life easy and go for a 15m circle. I am never bored, there is always something to correct or work on. It's really important to quash impatience and be happy with the small successes and progress.

Olympic level riders practice day in, day out, constantly honing, constantly improving, happy with the small successes, building on them day by day. You will be amazed at how much progress you will make by taking small steps and honing these increments.

In this chapter, I will be creating a series of tables with things you can and should be practicing, along with slightly harder variations. Clearly I won't be listing out every variation for every possible exercise, I just want to give you a flavor of the kind of steps and distances between steps you should be travelling along the training path.

Be careful what you practice even in between chunks of work you do within a session. The number of times I have to say to my daughter, when she is relaxing the horse in free walk after a session, that she should not allow the horse to fall in/out are beyond count! The horse spent the session well balanced and now in free walk catching her breath, she allows the horse to fall onto its shoulder. Does this seem tough? Yes for sure, but it's how bad habits form and in a short while any training can be undone.

Horses very quickly revert to old habits and patterns as quickly as they can learn new ones. I have been in the position of temporarily correcting a horse for a pupil, only to see the horse deteriorate before my very eyes within minutes as it matches it's patterns to the riders weaknesses. This is usually why when I school horses, I insist the rider has lessons over the schooling period so my fixes to the horse will be maintained by the rider.

In summary, you should strive to practice perfectly, a conscious attempt to improve against a well defined goal or standard. Here is a little test to see how well you focus. Find yourself a friend who will randomly call out 'now' during your schooling session. Every time they call out 'now' ask yourself how focussed you are. Did you zone out, did you just drift round the corner? Perhaps give yourself a number from 1 to 10. 1 would be not focussed at all, 10 would be completely absorbed in schooling.

Choosing NOT to practice perfectly

Sometimes we just have to accept the inevitable, that we can't 'fix' everything at once. Be this due to our skill level, or because the protective patterns the horse presents to you are too intractable. This can happen when we get a horse to ride which has habituated to certain patterns. A horse that hollows all the time, or rushes in its paces, or who is incredibly lazy and so on. Sometimes we have to choose to work on the worst problem and forget about some other problems for the time being.

Deliberately choosing to abandon efforts in some areas in order to fix a bigger problem can feel very weird especially when you are used to being able to handle multiple problems at once. When I school I can hold and track quite a few items at a time, rhythm, impulsion, feel of the horses back lifted, elastic contact and so on, and I can correct these things in real time. But there comes a point, when either your skill level or the horses patterns cause you to choose.

What then do we drop? What do we focus on instead? To what point in our training level do we retreat? It's very difficult to cover all situations and problematic patterns that the horse can throw at us, so I will cover some basic scenarios and some choices you can make. You may make less drastic retreats than I would, it depends on your skill level, your confidence, what you want to get out of riding your horse and so on. For instance, I am quite willing in some cases to retreat all the way back to ground work and lungeing to solve problems. This is because I am patient, but mostly I have the confidence of knowing that from the stage of groundwork and lungeing I can make sure progress. I can change the horses movement patterns without me riding it.

There is a lovely story Mary Wanless tells in her first book called 'Ride With Your Mind', where she explains she was training in France and she walked into the arena to find her teacher lungeing a horse with a very hollow back in side reins. The teacher said to her 'I lunge theese horse on zee lunge because eet ees not amusing for me to ride 'eem like thees'. This trainer had decided the sensible choice was all the way back to lungeing

Although lungeing and groundwork is rather beyond the scope of this book, it is an essential tool in your toolkit for training your horse. If you are the slightest bit worried, find a good trainer to teach you how, and show you the various ways for a horse to learn to reach down with its neck and lift up its back. I am a little reluctant to recommend tack, but I have had success with both side reins and also using a chambon, but you do need to know how to use them correctly.

Just from the above information, I think you can make the connection that I will tend to retreat to a point, where I can have the horse make the most progress. My thought process goes, what can I do to have the horse do the right thing, more of the time, so that it most quickly becomes a habit. I will now list a few examples:

Example Training Scenario.

Note - It goes without saying that the 'retreat' I talk about only occurs if one cannot find the skill to fix the issue - something we have all had to admit to, or at least should admit to, when evidence presents itself!

Horse is hollow in walk

I will attempt to teach the horse to lift its back with my seat (I often tip a little forwards and lighten my seat) and get it to stretch down into the rein in free walk on a long rein. Its seems to be something I am good at doing and really teaches the horse to stretch over its back and develop new patterns. If for whatever reason, I cannot even change the horses back shape in walk, I will retreat to lungeing the horse in side reins or a chambon. I will also get the horses back checked and perhaps have some physiotherapy done on the horse. I will make an assessment based on the horses muscle structure too. How habitual is this way of going for him and how much muscle wastage is there in the back? Assessing the muscle structure may show that I am wasting my time riding until I improve the horses muscles from lunge work.

Horse hollow in trot

Moving back to walk, will have established ability to get horse to stretch well in free walk on a long rein. Will attempt walk to trot transitions having the horse a little more stretched forward and down and attempt to move through walk to trot maintaining stretch. Patterning stretching in walk will help stretching in trot. Sometimes it is enough to ask the horse to stretch in trot once he understands it well in walk.

Horse falling in/out on circles in trot

I have sometimes been in a position where a horse is so crooked that once I make it into trot, I cannot prevent it falling in/out as well as I wish. In these cases I will walk and work on moving the horse in and out on circles, focussing on positioning the horses shoulder. For instance, should a horse fall in very badly, I will take it onto a circle and cause it to fall out for a short time (half a circle), so that it learns to move away from my inside leg. I find I only need to do this a few times and the horse begins to understand. On a 20m circle we should expect almost any horse to manage it without excessive falling in or out.

Horse against hand in walk-halt trans or trot-walk trans.

Generally this sorts itself quite quickly with normal training, but if it doesn't then ground work (known as Equine Learning Theory) based on the work of the Australian horse behaviour expert Andrew McLean solves this issue very quickly. The style of ground work, which teaches the horse to stop, go and park most accurately matches the aids used by the rider. I have used this technique before and seen amazing changes in the horse both on ground and whilst ridden. Mary Wanless offers coaching in the technique on all her courses.

The above solution also really goes for the following situations:

- Horse leaning on hand generally.
- Horse rushing (the horse becomes a lot more sensitive to the stop aids).
- Horse being lazy (horse learns to move away from the leg).
- Horse won't halt still for any period of time.
- Horse hollows (you can teach a horse to follow the contact using the Andrew McLean methods)

Photo 11

The above photos shows Tinker parking. Milly is able to walk around the horse in a semi-circle without the horse moving. This is an amazing training tool for horses which won't stand still in halt. You can progress to the point of asking the horse to halt, then running around the horse to the left and right whilst the horse remains parked. Initially, especially when Tinker got excited, she was very pushy coming out of her stable. This training made her so much easier to handle.

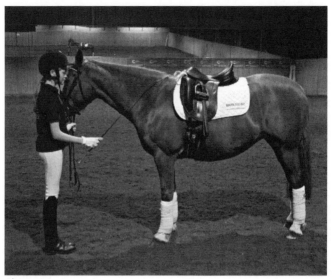

Photo 12

In the above photo Milly is desensitising Tinker to the whip. She will rub it slowly down her neck, shoulders, legs and so on. This is essential to being able to work with the horse without fear, and for it to have appropriate reactions to any taps or aids given with the stick.

Horse hollows in downward transitions.

Depending on your skill level, there are a number of fallback points. The furthest fallback point would be the ground work as previously mentioned. You could also work on it on the lunge. Typically I only have to go as far as walk to halt. I ask the horse to be a little more stretched into the rein, have its back more lifted up and then ease into the halt whilst lightening my seat slightly to encourage the back to stay up. I then do my best to keep the back lifted in the halt and walk on staying round. This doesn't seem to take too long to ingrain a pattern.

Running in medium trot

This comes down to the riders ability to maintain impulsion and create energy in trot. If your horse is running in medium trot, it usually means you don't have sufficient control of the trot tempo, whilst generating energy, to make medium trot happen. You will know when you are ready for medium trot, as it's a feeling you get, where your horse starts producing a little bit of cadence and you get the feeling that you have energy and power to spare. So the fall back point is actually your working trot, where you need to develop impulsion under tempo control.

Running into Canter / Incorrect Lead

This is usually caused by the rider and the aids they use. So do get some help, if you get into trouble with this, from a coach. If I was ever very stuck at this I would get the horse striking off into canter on command on the lunge first using a voice command. This could help when you get back on board. Check out the section on Understanding where I have some extra information on canter strike off.

Flat trot/ speedy trot

If you find yourself in trot getting little impulsion/cadence from the horse, it is worth returning to the use of trotting poles, as this helps teach the horse to flex its joints and give the rider a feel for the jump needed in trot work. It can also be used as a tool to steady the rushing trot tempo of a horse and get it to think more about itself.

Horse is somewhat distracted, or difficult to get to focus on the job.

The horse must pay attention, he must! In your own schooling arena your horse needs to be focused the whole time. I suggest people get a little primadonna about this. If you horse pricks his ears and bends his neck to the outside and looks up, he is definitely not paying attention to you! Ideally your horse would have his ears out sideways pretty much all of the time, totally absorbed in you and himself and in the game of dressage. Whatever it takes, inside leg, a little tickle with the whip, clicking of the tongue, clearing your throat, a growl or a bend to the inside.

Whilst mentioning inside bend, I tend to be averse to too much inside bend, as it simply causes the horse to fall onto its outside shoulder. However with a horse that is extremely distracted and doesn't listen to the rider, I will choose to forego absolute balance through the shoulder to get the horse to pay more attention. Once I increase the inside bend the horse is looking more to the inside of the circle and I will use circles and keep the inside bend to maintain attention. Attention seems to be habit-forming; one of the silly phrases I use when teaching is "the more they look, the more they look", so it is best to get into the habit of keeping the horse listening to you. In dressage, a horse looks inwards to concentrate on you and inwards on itself to maintain balance and focus on its own body.

At some point the horse learns to chew gum and talk at the same time. By this I mean that the horse can prick its ears and still manage to do perfectly well at responding to the riders aids and performing the movements. At this point I would never dream of telling the horse off or interfering, it simply means he developed the brain space to perform and perhaps slyly enjoy the scenery too!

Practicing for competitions

Practicing to get your horse used to competitions is really tough. There are several approaches you can take depending on your means. We try to take our horses out to other venues on non-competition days to hire out the school. We try to take more than one horse and often try to take a friend. This is a good way to begin to simulate a competition environment, a new place, travelling in the lorry, with less familiar horses but without the stress of a full-blown competition.

If you are at a yard where many horses share an arena, then get out of the habit of looking for a quiet slot! Get in there and warm up with two or three other horses at a minimum. Your main aim is to see how quickly you can get your horse listening to you and settled. The main stresses of a competition, are being at a new place in unfamiliar surroundings, surrounded by new horses which may or may not be well behaved! The closer you can come to simulating this environment the better. If you have an experienced friend it can be good to take your horse out to a showground, not to compete but merely to ride round and see the sights. Not every outing needs to be a competition and your goal is to get your horse used to different sights.

If you do not have easy access to a lorry or lack the funds to make many trips to different venues then perhaps your best bet is to find a trainer who specialises in desensitising horses. It can be quite empowering to be able to train your horse to ignore balloons, strange objects, noises and so on. A bombproof horse is worth its weight in gold!

Some next steps to take in training

Below is a small list designed to show the typical next steps I would think about, once my horse performed well in the 'current step'. I hadn't thought about it before, but as I write these words I wonder how I communicate what I consider to be 'good enough' before I will attempt the next level up. Personally my level would be 'a 7 in a dressage test'. If my horse can get a 7 in a dressage test for a certain movement, then I am happy to try the next item in the progression. Now obviously I don't wait until the dressage test before I decide, it's just the sort of level of competence I have in my own mind. I hope that helps!

Current Step	Next Step
Able to reach down into rein	Moving smoothly from free walk to medium walk and back
Good walk 20m/15m circles	Change of rein in walk through 2 half 10m circles.
Trot 20m circles	Trot 15m circles
Trot 15m circles	3 loop serpentines
3 loop serpentines	10m circles.
Change of rein across diagonal in trot	Change of rein in trot through 2 half 20m circles
Change of rein in trot	Change of rein in trot up the

through 2 half 20m circles	centre line, or from B to E
Change of rein in trot up the centre line, or from B to E	Half 10m circle and incline back to the track.
Leg yielding in walk	Demi pirouette in walk
Demi piroutte in walk	Shoulder in in walk
Trot walk transition	Trot halt transition
Balanced in downward transitions, consistent in outline and responsive to rein contact	Rein back

I specifically stayed away from collection and medium/extended paces as these are actually dependant on the capabilities of the horse, the level of impulsion and cadence the horse develops plus your own ability to maintain tempo throughout different levels of energy.

On Patience

A thoughtful patience will give you the greatest progress in dressage. Never be impatient to get onto the next movement, the next level or even the next pace. Making small progressions every day will get you there. I remember visiting Denmark whilst I was taking photographs for one of Mary's books and I was lucky enough to be photographing one of Mary's Grand Prix students, Heather Blitz. What was remarkable about Heather was her patience with the horses she was riding.

I remember one moment in particular where she was training one of the horses Piaffe. For the benefit of those watching she was explaining what she was thinking and what she was doing. The horse appeared to become a little tense and muddled and of this Heather said "now I would never try to interfere and tell this horse off, or somehow try to pressurise him because I can feel him trying underneath, I can feel him working it out, and I know that this is a process he has to go through". Now I am somewhat paraphrasing Heather here because it was a long time ago and I can't remember her exact words so I hope she will forgive me if I was unable to directly quote her. Back to the story, sure enough the horse began to relax and take better steps.

One of the things worth remembering when training your horse, especially if you are learning to, that this is just as strange for him as it is for you. Both horse and rider must learn new neurological patterns and change existing ones. They must both learn new habits and break old ones. The rider has the luxury of both knowing the reason for these changes and has the ability to choose them. The horse on the other hand is simply trying to do what it is being told in an attempt to please the rider; he has no idea why this is happening or why he feels strange. Listening to Heather explain her thinking almost brought tears to my eyes because it showed a deep understanding and empathy for her horse. So it is worth remembering that should your horse get confused, or a little tense, or finds something difficult, it's not a moment for additional pressure or punishment, but some reassurance in recognition of how strange this must be for him and how you appreciate his efforts.

Off the horse

This is not relevant for everyone, some people are born calm and act calm naturally. However, in this day and age of high stress, high power jobs, you may find yourself a little highly strung, or perhaps you are naturally this way inclined. I tend so see riders who are highly strung act a little quickly or perhaps jerkily around their horses. Their manner too abrupt, and their movements too quick. This can easily transmit itself to the horse, who is naturally nervous of quick movements. It is almost as if their thoughts are too quick, and everything happens at double time.

Learning to move smoothly around horses is what I call 'schooling your actions', and whilst on top I call it 'schooling your reactions'. Mostly because on top we are responding to feedback from the horse, and on the ground we are 'doing' things. I was recently talking with Sue Palmer about this very thing, and she told me that Monty Roberts says to "move as if through treacle" when working around horses. This sounds like a really good description!

My basic point here, is that when moving around your horse, when handling them, when tacking them up and so on, you need to control the speed of your limbs so that there is no suddenly acceleration of them – like Monty's moving through treacle. When you hand reaches up to remove the bridle, school your actions, when you go to pat your horse, school your actions. I think you get it now. But the point of this being in the section on practice, is that this does need some practice! I now do this naturally but I do have to tell my daughter now and again to remember this!

This idea also has its place whilst riding too. When I am teaching the horse to follow my hand in free walk on a long rein, I can give the rein in such a smooth manner that it doesn't loop and the horse continues to seek it. When changing bend, moving from walk to trot and changing diagonal you must be smooth in your actions and reactions. I have seen people react far to quickly with the hand if the horse were to raise his head; that is also a place to learn to school your reactions.

Many of us have been through the phase of thinking with our hands too much. I remember clearly a day when I had a breakthrough and realised I had learned something pretty monumental. I was trucking along in trot when suddenly the horse raised its head slightly… gasp, horror… and I did NOTHING. Its head went back down, its back came up and on we went. I just didn't feel the urgent need to interfere, I knew it would correct by itself. What a moment that was, and it made me smile a lot. I realised I had got to the stage where I was confident in my training and riding, that I could choose not to react. I had schooled my reactions!

What is going on inside your head?

An interesting question? This is really about how it is you talk to yourself when you ride and how you 'coach' yourself when you ride. What is your internal chatter like when you ride?

Do you hear your own coach talking at you, reminding you what to do? Do you hear an internal voice critiquing yourself as you ride round? How supportive is the voice in your head? Is there more chatter when things are going wrong and less when its going right? What happens on those days when you get a really good ride, is there less chatter?

From the days when you begin to learn to ride, there seems endless details that you must remember. Inside leg here, outside leg there, sit up, use the inside rein, don't tip forwards, look to your next marker and so on. I think its quite easy to get into the habit of speaking to yourself in your mind in very longwinded ways, which take so much time, that by the time you start saying it, the moment has past.

Changes in balance, position, movement, place in the arena and pace all happen extremely quickly and from moment to moment. There simply isn't time when riding to give yourself a lecture, bemoan how badly you did the last movement or transition, or congratulate yourself on how well you did something. Riding well requires huge amounts of focus, and requires focus from moment to moment without the rider absenting themselves from the process by complex internal dialogue.

If you must remind yourself of some correction that you need to make then try to reduce it down to one or two words only. Examples could be 'hands up', 'bear down', 'breath', 'leg back', 'look up' and so on. Mine currently are 'bear down', 'back chain', 'seat bones back', 'tempo' and 'rein length'. When I get unfit I have a situation where my front ends up being shorter than my back, so I will be tipping forwards too much with a round back and my seat bones pointing a little to forward. So I build up a little check list of super short phrases that I can say to myself.

Go ahead now, put down the book, get yourself a piece of paper and try to write down all things you currently have to think about when you ride. Write down the corrections you have to make, the issues your horse has, and so on. After you have done this, see if you can write down some very short phrases that would remind you of what you need to do or remember. Next time you ride, make a conscious effort to cut down the chatter and deploy your short helpful phrases.

Keeping down the internal chatter this way makes you much more focused in the here and now and much less likely to start berating yourself and thereby absenting yourself from the present. If you do catch yourself making unhelpful criticism a great thing to think to yourself is 'Next!' and then try to re-engage with what's happening and move onto the next helpful thought.

When schooling a students horse, I can usually talk about what I am working on, and what challenges the horse is presenting to me. Notice I didn't say that I talked about 'what I am thinking about' because there isn't much 'thought' going on up there. Let me take a recent example for you below, and I will talk you through the process. You may be surprised by what I tell you! I hope from my description below, you can see that trying to tell yourself all of this would just take way too long!

Inside my head!

The horse was very "whizzy" and I could feel myself getting taken off with in walk. I was having trouble controlling the horses footsteps. I was focusing on stabilising my torso and reducing how much the horse was swinging around my pelvis and seat bones so that I could get control of the tempo. I noticed that not only did the horses movement try to "jiggle" me around in the saddle, but also that the movement continued up my spine into my chest. I noticed that as I got control of my seat bones and reduced how much wiggle there was, and prevented it from travelling up to my chest, I was able to slow the tempo of the walk down.

The horse had a particular pattern that meant it would attempt a 'take over bid' so that it could speed off again, by taking hold of the rein. I think it expected the rider to take hold too and set up a pattern where it would lengthen the underside of it's belly, hollow and speed off out in front. I had to stay focused so that when it tried to come against the hand, I had a momentary block but then gave the contact momentarily and refused to get involved in a pulling match, and also just kept focusing on controlling my seatbones and staying stable, not getting pulled out of shape by the horse. I was also attempting to draw the horses back up underneath me and I monitored the horses attention level too. I noticed that when the horse attempted a take over bid, it would often lose attention and prick its ears.

This horse required a huge amount of focus from me as a rider and I think you will agree that the largest amount of my attention was on 'noticing'. What was the horse doing to me, what was I doing to it, what patterns was the horse setting up. Now at no time was all of this verbalized inside my head, it was mainly a cycle of noticing, correcting, noticing and correcting. I was saying things like 'chest', 'sit stiller' but even then I don't think there was even time. Notice and correct, notice and correct – there isn't much time for discussing, critisising, worrying or congratulating yourself. Actually one further little tip I can give you, for when it goes wrong, or when you make a mistake. Don't sweat it! I tend to say 'oops' or 'sorry' and move on. The sorry is usually to the horse! This is a great attitude to take with you into competition. If I make a mistake when I am competing, I find it momentarily amusing, its shaken off and I refocus back into the moment. Do not attach much weight to mistakes, learn from them, move on and put them behind you.

What level of achievement can you expect?

I think a gentle level of progress, to say novice level in dressage can be achieved in a year. Novice level appears to equate to First level in USA. Some horses and riders can achieve this more quickly but a year is good amount of time. It gives the horse time to develop muscle, balance and experience competing. The purpose of giving a time period like this, is that if it is taking a lot longer (let's say two years) to make the progress and you have the ambition to want to achieve more, you should look for some professional help and assessment. See the chapter on Review!

Clearly it can take longer than a year if you don't have the time to ride, or the facilities, or need to work a lot on your own skill level. But training your horse 5-6 days a week, with some slightly longer periods off work (perhaps a month of rest in the year) then you shouldn't have trouble making Novice level. I have seen it take much less time to get to Novice, but as I mentioned this depends on the skill level of the rider and horse.

It is worth saying that only very skillful professional riders with very good horses take about 5 years to get to Grand Prix level. Since there are 11 levels to Grand Prix in the UK, then one could say 2-3 levels a year. For most people progress will inevitably slow once you get towards medium level in dressage unless you have a horse capable of more. Any uncompromised horse should be able to make it to medium level.

Daily progress

What I want to see each day, is a little progress. I feel the horse 'get' what I want, become more consistent, require less corrections, begin to improve their strength and progress smoothly through the levels.

Each training session for me, is as long as it takes to achieve what I want without over-tiring the horse. Luckily for my horse I am easily pleased! Speaking more seriously I would say 45minutes is a nice length of training session with a maximum of an hour. I occasionally have outliers to this continuum where a session may go on for longer, or be quite a bit shorter, but 45minutes feels right.

I find it very easy to know when my horse isn't right. Plus I would rather give my horse the benefit of the doubt. Rarely is a horse suddenly stiffer, or more resistant to go forwards, or displaying other unusual behavior without a reason. Perhaps the horse worked really well the previous session, but now seems stiff... or it is suddenly pushing back at you in upward or downward transitions. My first thoughts when something like this happens are "I wonder what's going on here", I try to use my skill to ride through it but if the horse is insistent then it's time to look at tack, muscle stiffness, pulled muscle and so on. It never takes the horse long to convince me something isn't right. For some riders this may be a difficult call, to know if your horse is kidding you, or if there is something really going on. Getting someone to video the issue can help too. If a quick 'Oy!' to the horse doesn't rectify the situation, it's worth looking at.

Boredom

I am wary when a rider or pupil claims that they can't get enough practice in their flat work because their horse gets bored. Generally for a horse to get bored or stale, it will either be because it is being ridden in a way which unknowingly invokes resistance and tension on a continued basis, or because the work is done in a very unfocused way.

When a horse is being trained correctly, it is totally focused on the rider and its work, so there is no room for boredom or staleness, especially if the horse is being challenged in the right way. The same goes for the rider, when the rider is focused and involved in the process, time flies. If you find yourself unfocussed, or not sure what you should be doing, then it's a sign there is a hole in your training program and learning.

However, we should do new things! Go out for a ride, take a trip to another venue and so on. It's all the part of the horses education, all which will prevent 'boredom' - though I don't know on whose part! I have never personally had a horse get bored of training, even with limited riding out, though I am lucky enough to have access to an indoor arena, an outdoor arena and a lorry to take the horse to different venues.

Practice Tests

Dressage practice days are an excellent introduction to competing and offer valuable feedback on the progress you are making. The format differs only very slightly from venue to venue but in essence you are able to book a slot to do a test and then receive feedback from a judge. Often the venue then allows you to redo the test with the new information the judge has provided and hopefully get a better score.

Practice days are generally a lot less stressful than real competitions, they usually have much fewer people attending and much more relaxed. At our venue we provide a 30 minute slot for each competitor, so as you can imagine there are only usually two or three people warming up at most. First the rider performs the test of their choice, then they receive feedback from the judge in a 15 minute coaching session. Whenever I run these training sessions I always ask the person at the end of the initial coaching whether they would like to redo the test or continue the coaching to the end. It is very rare that somebody chooses to do the second test but rather finds the extra coaching valuable and don't see the point in tiring the horse by doing another test.

Practice tests are a great way to review your progress, especially if you are doing these at the same venue time and time again. Usually the judge is pretty flexible in the advice they can offer you. When judging a person for the first time I try and decide what will help them the most.

This could be helping them with their test riding technique, or it could be that some basic biomechanics of the horse or rider are affecting the test results more than anything else. Practice days when done well will seem like a mixture of competing and having a coaching session.

Customers at our equestrian centre also go away with a rosette!

Learning dressage tests

Forgetting your test in the middle of a competition can be very upsetting and cause loss of confidence. I use two ways of remembering a test. Both of them do rely upon a knowledge of the markers and their place in the arena. This is something you should get used to visualising so you can picture the arena in your minds eye and know where the letters sit in relation to each other.

The first involves walking it out in an area with similar proportions to the arena, perhaps the living room floor. Go through your test sheet and try to remember the first few movements. Practice them on foot in the area you put aside, trying to think about how you would take the horse through each movement. Gradually add on each movement until you can get from beginning to the end without a mistake. The mind remembers stories best, so make sure you think about the journey through the test and all the ways you have to think of preparing your horse.

The second method is using mental rehearsal, which I talk about in the chapter Review. Close your eyes and imagine yourself riding your horse through the test. Not just watching yourself, but feeling what it would feel like to be on the horse, then make your way around the test, making the changes of bend, of pace and so on. I often use this one directly after I have walked it out physically on the ground.

My 'secret' method to remembering all kinds of tests will be revealed to you through one the weekly webinars you get access to; for details look out for the special offer page found on page 191. I am not excluding it to be mean, it is because this method will probably take a webinar to explain, and its only really for people who compete a lot who will be doing multiple tests. In fact by the end of the webinar, everyone should have memorized two example tests we will be using.

Improving your feel through practice

Having someone on the ground and having the right questions asked of you can make a huge difference to how quickly you learn feel. Feel is simply the ability to differentiate between various levels of input. One section that made me laugh when reading one of Mary Wanless's books was when she said that when she looks back at how she used to ride, she realised it was like riding under anaesthetic. Developing feel is making yourself sensitive to the changes that are happening underneath you, to the changes that are happening in yourself and then being able to choose correct reactions to these changes.

Here is an example of a great way to develop feel for how much impulsion you should have. It does require initially a person on the ground to help calibrate what you feel with what they see. The technique I'm about to explain is credited to Mary Wanless.

If we take a scale from 1 to 10, five is in the middle representing perfect power with perfect rhythm. Six, seven, eight, nine, ten represent the horse progressively getting faster and faster and more out of control. Four, three, two, one represent the horse losing energy and getting slower and slower. So in one scenario we have energy but no tempo control, and in the other scenario we have tempo control but no energy. Have the person on the ground randomly say "now" and when they do give a number from the top of your head which describes the feeling you have about the level of impulsion and power.

It may be that when the person says now, you say it is 4.5 when it might actually be a 3. This is why it's important to have the person on the ground calibrate you to the correct number. I find that very quickly the rider calibrates and begins speaking the right numbers to describe the level of impulsion. Once you get this number system it is something you can ask yourself frequently, as you are competing or schooling. The number off the top of your head will become quite accurate and is a great guide.

Here is another great exercise to develop feel. Once again credit must go to Mary. Teaching rider biomechanics is beyond the scope of what I can teach here, so I will state how the seat bones move in walk and if yours move differently then have a look at the resources section at the end of the book where you will be able to find a video explaining this.

In walk the left seat bone goes forward and then the right seat bone move forwards and then the left seat bone moves forward and then the right seat bones forward, kind of like bottom walking, like when babies shuffle along on their bottoms one side at a time. If you find this hard, try to notice how the horse moves your knees to begin with; can you feel your knees being moved left, right by the horses movement, then perhaps can you feel your thighs being moved separately left and right by the horse, then finally each side of your hips and then on to your seat bones.

If you correctly have the idea of your seat bones moving, you can then begin to know which hind leg is coming underneath you at any given point. For instance when your left seat bone is back and about to come forwards the horses left hind leg will be travelling forwards. Again you are going to need somebody on the ground to help you with this. You should probably call now every time the seat bone is back and about to come forwards. Then have the person on the ground verify that you are calling it as the hind leg is moving forwards.

The numbering system mentioned previously can be used in many ways, from labelling impulsion, to verifying how focused you are as a rider. I have used it to improve riders focus on their breathing, on how upright they are, to how aware they stay through difficult movements and the straightness of the horse. Developing feel is not a mystery and is not only available to the talented. Feel can be developed by improving the riders ability to focus, giving them something to focus on and educating them on what the different feels means and what their responses should be.

Planning your schooling

I often get asked if I plan my schooling sessions. The truthful answer to this is 'yes' and 'no'. In general, from the previous session, I obviously know what stage my horse is at in its training. I know what needs working on, and how I will go about working on it. However I do not enter the arena and begin drilling my horse in whatever it is I want him to improve upon. We have a warm up, we practice simpler exercises to establish the horse at his current level and then we may move onto what it is I would like to work on.

I am not at all attached to my plan in the schooling session. I am not in the slightest bit bothered if I do not get to work on what I wanted and find out I need to re-establish some other habit into the horse. For instance the horse may be stiff, or perhaps it has developed a straightness issue, or some other fault – I drop the plan without a second thought and work on these other things.

Having a plan when coming out to school is having an awareness for the next steps that are lying out there on the horizon in the horse's training. If the conditions are right, we will attempt them, if not we don't mind.

My warm up routine is almost always the same. I do not vary it hardly at all. I want the horse to have this routine become a habit, something soothing, something to fall back on. The only time I ever vary is if the horse for some reason is too excitable to stretch, relax and pay attention immediately. I would then work it in medium walk for a while, getting it to pay attention and work a little. Invariably then after a little bit of work, it is happy to stretch.

The warm up for a novice horse becomes:

- free walk on a long rein both directions
- changes of rein in walk moving from free walk on a long rein to medium walk. This teaches the horse to relax its frame and move softly between free and medium.
- walk 10m circles and changes of rein through half 10m circles
- walk – halt transitions.
- Moving up into trot – soft, round but not at full impulsion so the horse has a chance to ease out stiffness.
- 20m circles at A, E, C and B
- Some stretching in trot on the circles
- Changes of rein across the diagonal
- Some small amount of canter work.

After this warm up the horse has a small rest and I am then ready to begin some more challenging work with it. How do you warm up your horse? What are you trying to achieve with your warm up? What can you tell about how your horse feels, what mood he is in, and what physical shape he is in? A good warm up can tell you an awful lot about your horse.

Peter Dove

8 REVIEW

I believe review to be the main missing element for most people who are training their horses and themselves for dressage. In fact in most cases, it takes place for about 10 minutes upon receiving a dressage test and ends shortly after that.

I hope that in this chapter you will get a taste for review and that you will see how beneficial it is to your progress. It's easy to say, "I don't have time", but the question is, do you really want what's best for you and your horse? I am sure that answer is a resounding "Yes", so hopefully you will make the time for review in its many forms and become a rider who works to become better whether they are off their horse or on their horse. I think also you will be surprised by how little time you would need to do this review.

Tools For Review

Here are the main tools for review that I use.

- Video
- Mental Rehearsal/Review
- Test Sheets
- Spreadsheets
- Coaches/Friends
- Riding Journal
- Mirrors

Over the course of this chapter I will expand upon each of these tools and explain what you should be looking for in each of them. Each has their own strengths and uses, some can be done on the horse and some off the horse, so there is something for everyone.

Video

For some of you video may seem something of an obvious tool to suggest. Of course video you say! With the advent of mobile phones and tablets capable of doing an OK job of videoing at a reasonable quality, I often see people videoing with an iPad in our arena gallery. However, I am not sure riders do a very scientific job of analyzing the results of their videoing efforts, or even give more than a cursory look at the resulting video. In this section I would like to show what you could be looking for and what you could learn from the video.

The most obvious thing to do is to match up the mark and the comment you got from the judge with the video section of you performing the movement. Does the mark match with your opinion of the movement? Does the comment make any sense? Are you able to relate to it? Can you see anything else that went wrong, that was not mentioned on the sheet? I recommend that you get used to rewinding the video to see the same section over several viewings. You spent so long getting to the venue, that you might as well pick every piece of experience and learning you can from it.

As well as looking at the errors, try to review what you were doing well. What looked the smoothest and where were you most accurate?

In the chapter on fluidity I mentioned that fluidity mostly came from those moments between movements. How you flowed from one movement to the next, how bend changes from one moment to the next, how smooth transitions were, how balanced your horse stays and how consistent you were. Take the time to look through the video and focus on those moments. Can you pick out movements when your horse looked unprepared for the movement and can you pick out where you didn't prepare for a transition or a turn?

What about your own riding? Check yourself out when you ride away from the camera. Were you straight, or do you lean one way or another? How quiet do you look as a rider? How did you react when things went wrong? Do you look different, or ride differently to how you do when you are home?

Look at the rhythm and tempo of the horse. Does this stay constant throughout a movement? What about coming out of canter into trot, how long does it take to establish a good rhythm? Look at his energy levels, do they remain the same? Do his energy levels change depending on the size of the circle, or perhaps as you move laterally?

How consistent is your horse's outline? Does he remain steady to the contact, or is he unsettled? Does he drop his poll too deep in places, perhaps in downward transitions, or hollow in upward transitions? Is his nose still as he comes towards the camera, or is there any side to side swinging?

How straight was your horse in each of the paces? Is there any wobble on the centre line? Does he have his quarters to one side or the other? What about in canter, is he doing quarters in? Is he showing more inside bend than normal, perhaps falling onto the inside shoulder? What happens in lateral work, does the positioning of the forehand or quarters change?

And finally, does your horse track up or over track in the appropriate movements? When you do medium trot, can you detect over track and how much ground cover occurs? Does free walk on a long rein produce more over track than in the medium walk?

Before you run shrieking at the large number of questions and the enormous amount to think about, remember that some of this will be answered through the judges' comments for you and some of it will be obvious to you. However to make things easier I have created a checklist, available on the next few pages and on my website for download, that you can use when reviewing video. It is slightly more comprehensive than this chapter and is a handy reminder to have around. In fact anytime you want to review your progress, it can give you some ideas as to what you should be checking! We often have so many things on our minds that this falls off the end of our lists easily! I have tried repeating myself as much as possible, since some things can be applied no matter what you are working on such as tempo, outline and impulsion.

Please excuse the pigeon English within the checklist, I tried to keep everything on a single line.

Circles/Turns, does remain balanced through both shoulders?	
Circles/Turns, does maintain impulsion?	
Circles/Turns, does maintain outline?	
Circles/Turns, does show suppleness when changing bend?	
Transitions Down, does remain in an outline?	
Transitions Down, does not fall onto forehand?	
Transitions Down, transition is smooth and not abrupt?	
Transitions Down, horse moves smoothly away in new pace?	
Transitions Down, doesn't lose energy after transition?	
Transitions Down, isn't against hand?	
Transitions Down, remains straight?	

Transitions Up, does outline remain consistent?	
Transitions Up, does horse move smoothly to next pace?	
Transitions Up, does the horse remain straight?	
Medium Trot, does show over-track?	
Medium Trot, does maintain same tempo as in working trot?	
Medium Trot, does lengthen frame slightly?	
Medium Trot, does remain in a good outline?	
Lateral work, does maintain a consistent positioning?	
Lateral work, does show correct bend?	
Lateral work, does maintain smooth tempo and true rhythm?	
Canter, horse is not quarters in.	
Canter, horse is not falling onto outside shoulder on straight.	
General, horse is not too deep in outline.	
General, horse has no side to side movement in head.	
General, is horse steady to the contact?	
General, in the give and retake does horse remain balanced?	

General, in the give and retake does maintain outline or hollow?	
In walk, is there a true 4 time beat?	
In medium walk, is there an over-track and activity?	
In working trot, does the horse track up?	
Does move freely forwards, or is rider pushing all the time?	
Simple change through walk, remain straight or quarters swing?	
Free walk on long rein, does take contact forward + down?	
Free walk on long rein, does have more over-track and be active?	
Stretching in trot, does tempo remain same, does stretch down?	
Halt, is square?, is straight?, does remain attentive,? steps back?	
Leg yield, does stay straight? Do quarters get left behind?	
Demi-pirouette walk, does hind feet keep stepping in time?	
Demi-pirouette walk, does hind feet keep stepping in time?	
Medium canter, shows longer strides within same tempo?	
Medium canter, does show smooth transitions into and out of?	
2 half 10m circles change rein, shows an instant of straightness?	

There are clearly many more things you could be asking yourself as you watch your test. This list will get you into the habit of being a little bit more critical and observant of your test, so that learning does not slip you by.

Mental Rehearsal/Review

Mental rehearsal was a discipline introduced to me by Mary Wanless, in her first book "The Natural Rider" or as it is known in the UK as "Ride With Your Mind". In mental rehearsal one aims to imagine oneself riding the previous session as if you were actually riding the horse, not viewing yourself as a third person, but feeling what you were feeling and hopefully seeing what you are seeing.

Suppose you had a problem in the previous session, you should try to imagine yourself riding the problem and then visualise yourself doing it correctly using a memory for when it went well. You can take this to a more advanced level by mentally editing the session and replacing all of the problem areas with visualisations of you doing it correctly. The brain cannot tell the difference between you imagining it happening and it actually happening, insomuch that the neurological pathways still get strengthened in a similar way as if you were actually practising. You will notice this as you do your visualisation, as you will feel your muscles responding to the visualisation.

I remember having many breakthroughs after I have ridden by using mental rehearsal. One particular instance was when I had a more advanced horse to ride which could easily do lateral movements and all kinds of "fancy stuff". The horse was a little stiff and fairly old and I was having trouble with canter in that the horse was bringing its quarters in. The trouble was the more I tried to correct the problem the more the quarters went in and I was getting pretty frustrated with myself.

I knew that I should have my inside seat bone in advance and my outside seat bone back. Somehow in my brain, in order to get this back to a true canter I was emphasising my inside seat bone in advance and my outside seat bone back. Imagine how silly I felt, upon doing some mental rehearsal, to realise the fact that when the horse brings his quarters in he is moving my inside seat bone even more forward and my outside seat bone even more back! So in fact my corrections were making it even worse, my horse was putting my inside seat bone too far forward and I was helping along the way!

As soon as I drew the inside seat bone back to a more correct place and advance the outside seat bone, the horse began to straighten up. In fact I was positioning myself and the horse more for shoulder in and that is indeed the correction required for fixing a horse whose quarters come in at canter. Perhaps if I had done my mental rehearsal earlier, rather than waited until I was really frustrated, I would have learned that bit quicker!

Mental rehearsal can not only improve your riding, but it can also improve your teaching. I have many a time reviewed a lesson this way and worked out a better way of helping the rider.

Test Sheets

This is a pretty obvious one, but I still believe people miss out on getting the most benefit from reading test sheets. Some of these points were made in the video section, so I will avoid repeating where possible.

The first question you should ask yourself is 'Do the comments match my expectations?'. These days, I am never surprised by the comments on a sheet, or by the marks. However, when starting out and even to quite an experienced level, you can still be surprised. This can be for a number of reasons and in the final wrap up of this chapter I will go through some of them.

You also want to be asking yourself whether the marks match up to your expectations? I tend to ask the comments question first because marks can fluctuate between judges, between venues and whether you are at an affiliated or unaffiliated competition. Marks can be affected by the surface you are riding on! Still, the marks should at least be relative, if your trot work is better than your canter, you would expect better marks there. Note any mark that surprises you, why it surprises you and then perhaps check on the video, or ask the judge.

Talk to the judge where possible about anything you are unsure about. Most judges I know are happy to help out and explain. Sometimes they won't remember your test specifically, after judging 40+ horses, however they may remember you, or at the very least they will explain the comment and what it means.

Talk to your trainer, ask them to look at the test. Are they surprised by anything on the sheet? I have seen comments on sheets of pupils which I know will be there, because the pupil has not yet got to the stage of being able to solve an issue. So it's reassuring to hear from the trainer, that they know about the issue and it's something you will tackle at some point when both horse and rider are ready.

One thing I would say, is that getting negative comments can be a little hurtful to our pride, especially if we are not expecting them and don't understand them. For instance, you may believe that your horse is doing medium trot, but your comments say 'running' or 'no difference shown', and get quite annoyed at the judge believing you are doing it correctly! Never dismiss a judges comment out of hand. It might be easy to say 'they always say that' or 'they don't know what they are talking about' or 'she doesn't like my horse'. The truth of the matter may be that you misunderstand the requirements of the movement, or perhaps underestimate some aspect of the requirements.

An example would be free walk on a long rein. You may give your reins and your horse would relax a little and you may think he is free and showing good relaxation. However, if your horse does not stretch forward and down to the contact, increase the amount of over track in the walk and remain straight, you will get low marks. It is vital to understand the purpose and requirements of the movements. If in doubt then ask!

The Spreadsheet

Spreadsheets? For Horses? What will the world come to next? Well for one, we are all busying around with iPad videoing our horses, so a little more software technology is not too out of place.

This method is simpler than it sounds, if you know how to use a spreadsheet. I also include a link on my website, where you can download the spreadsheet for yourself.

Firstly, this method works well when you are doing 3 or 4 tests in a short space of time and all at a similar level. Down the left hand side of the spreadsheet, the Y axis, you list all of the typical movements found in the tests you are doing. This includes circles, turns, transitions, lateral movements and so on. Across the top, on the X axis, you have repeated groups of the following headings: Date, Comment and Mark. It is possible to add in Venue if you are doing a lot of competitions and you get different comments or marks depending on venue.

Then, after competing and getting together 3 or 4 test sheets, begin entering the information into the columns provided. The idea here is simple,as we would like to see if we get similar comments and marks for specific movements within the test. You are looking for patterns, such as:

1. Do we get higher or lower marks for different paces.
2. Do we get penalized on specific circle sizes or

movements.

3. Is there a difference depending on which rein we are on?
4. Is there a theme in the comments among similar movements such as downward transitions, upward transitions or circles?
5. What do we tend to score highly on?

These items will be easy to see, for all we need to do is look at a movement, let's say circle right 10m diameter, then look across the spreadsheet at the 3 or 4 comments and marks we got for it.

Not only can you use the spreadsheet to analyse areas for you to work on, but you can also begin seeing improvement and progression over a period of time.

Movement	Prelim 4 20th Jan 2014		Prelim 18 23rd Jan 2014		
	Mark	Comment	Mark	Comment	Ma
20M Circle Left	6	Losing outside shoulder	6	Circle too big	
20M Circle Right	7	Fair Rhythm	8		
Up Center Line	6	needs more suppleness	5	losing balance on turn	
Change rein FXH	7		7		
Change rein KXM	7		6	lose balance at K	
Canter Trans Left	6	late to strike off	6		
Canter Trans Right	7		7		
Walk to trot	8	Smooth trans	7	Needs a little more energy	
Halt	6	Not square	6	Distracted	
Free Walk On A Long Rein	7	Could march on more	6	Needs more ground cover	

Photo 13 – example layout

Coaches and Friends

Getting a coach to review your current state of riding is a very useful type of lesson to have. In this type of lesson the instructor can put you through your paces, observe how you will perform, adjust the exercises to help highlight your strong and weak points and then provide an assessment at the end. I prefer to provide the assessment both verbally and written, so that we have a chance to sit down at the end of the session and discuss rather than trying to hold it all in memory.

It is also good if the session can be videoed, because the assessment can be backed up through sections on the video and pointed out in the debriefing at the end. This kind of training session dedicated to making an assessment should be done every 3 to 6 months depending on how many lessons you have and the frequency with which you ride.

Making progress and getting help doesn't always require a coach. Friends, family, husbands and wives all make great coaches whether they know it or not! They don't even need to be particularly horsey, they just have to be able to answer questions honestly. You can give the most basic of training such as teaching them to see if your horse is tracking up or explaining the correct outline so they can tell you if your horse is overbent or above the bridle, or being able to tell you whether your circle shapes are actually circular and so on. After this they will be able to help you immensely. If you remember the chapter on practice, they can be a great help in setting up the circle shapes in the arena and gleefully telling you when you are falling off one side of the other of the shapes.

Riding Journal

Keeping a riding journal can prove useful in a number of ways. Firstly just purchase any diary or notepad that you can set aside to use for this purpose. It even helps if you make it a rather nice, more expensive notebook, as this means you are much more likely to use it! The idea is to make notes each time you ride or train your horse.

You should take note of the day and date and what time you rode. You can even make note of the weather, the venue, the surface you rode on, any changes in tack. Write down how you felt physically and emotionally. Make notes on anything that went really well and also make note of any issues you came across, how you solved them and take note if you needed to seek any help.

Once a week you can review the previous week, look for any repeating issues or patterns and check for anything that you were supposed to follow up on and forgot about. If you are having regular lessons you can always check your journal before going to your lesson in case it reminds you of anything you need to ask.

Finally the biggest benefit of having a riding journal is that it does reinforce the fact that progress is made and things are getting better. We humans acclimatise to change very quickly, so we often forget how far we've come and often get bogged down in the here and now issues.

Here is an example of an entry I made – minus date/time:

"Rode Tinker today for 15 minutes before Milly got on. Attempting to help her prepare for the Team Quest Champs. Mare being much straighter through her shoulders now. Have to really keep a level of attention on my left leg otherwise it loses stillness. Noticed that as I get tired I tend to tip. Tinker didn't lean at all today on hand, except when she thought it was time to canter and then it was more of a fall on forehand than a lean. Corners are much more balanced now, time to start thinking about doing three loop serpentines and 15m circles to challenge her balance"

Arena Mirrors

If you are lucky enough to have mirrors in your indoor arena, then do keep looking up and using them. I use them to get an instant view of what is happening. Maybe this short section should have been in the chapter on Practice but it landed here instead. A form of instant review and feedback.

If you don't have mirrors then it might be worth investing in some panels. Our arena has one short side fully paneled with mirrors, however if I were just to start out again I would begin with a few panels set up like so.

I would have one panel at the end of a long side, so that if I were riding down the long side, I would see my horse straight on. This is really great for checking straightness in both the horse and yourself.

Then I would have 2 or 3 panels on the short side, so that if I were doing a circle at E or B I could look across and check out what we looked like sideways on. Sideways checks are good for seeing the outline of the horse, how much impulsion it has and how consistent it is.

Review at a high level

Whilst we have talked about some specific things to look for when performing a review, I would like to cover at a high level all of the elements you need to look for and why they are so important to our five-step process.

I believe accuracy to be the starting point for improving your marks at dressage, so when you are reviewing your test sheets, your journal, your lessons and so on you should be checking on how well you are doing with your accuracy. Without accuracy you cannot improve upon your fluidity.

The next element you should be checking is your fluidity, check your video, check your comments, look in the mirror, ask your trainer and make sure that you are getting those fluid changes of bend, smooth transitions and making correct use of the arena.

The next stage is to have a look at your understanding, as this often becomes obvious when you are struggling with certain issues, or perhaps when your expectation of marks and comments on your test sheet is different to what you have received. Never be satisfied with not understanding a comment or mark, seek out the judge, seek out your trainer, do some research online or find a book by an author you respect. If you are having trouble training your horse at home with some specific issue, then get it videoed and ask some friends, check with your trainer and analyse how you are tackling the situation, perhaps using mental rehearsal.

Have a look on my website and you will find a section where you can submit a video of you riding and ask a specific question. I will do my best to answer your question. This service is only available for people who have purchased my book, as you will be asked to enter a word on a specific page of the book before you are given access to the area.

Finally from all the above elements you can start to understand what it is you need to practice. Not only will this change what you are currently practicing, but perhaps your new understanding will help you practice more efficiently and cause you to review your own training sessions.

A long time ago, in the mists of time, I used to get on the horse without much idea of what we were going to work on. I would try a bit of this, or a bit of that because that's what I thought we 'ought' to be able to do by now.

I came across a horse that was so hollow that I couldn't

get it to stay round through transitions and it was pretty frustrating to say the least. (In those days I had little patience!). It occurred to me to try and teach the horse to go long and low, to stretch over its back in an attempt to change it muscle structure and build a different pattern into him. After he had learned to stretch in walk and actually really enjoy stretching at will, I decided I would teach it to him in trot too. To cut a long story short, I eventually taught the horse to stay round through transitions by increasing the level of stretch I was asking for just before the transition and allowing him to take a little longer to move from walk to trot.

The point of the story is that this learning, completely reshaped how I school horses and what I practice. Whenever I begin schooling a horse now, we have quite a consistent warm up. We spend time in walk, stretching on each reinand I then start changing the rein in walk, both going from medium to free walk and back again. Once I have been through this, the horse has done some gentle stretching and is ready to move into a trot. I rarely vary this start to warming up and it has served me well. Some people may tell you not to spend long in walk as it may ruin the horses walk, but I think that is only an issue if you are asking too much in the walk at the start, perhaps over collecting your horse and causing excessive tension. I have never had anything but positive things come out of this warm up ritual.

I hope you can see how a review of each of the different levels feed into each other. Looking at accuracy will help your fluidity, a study of issues in accuracy and fluidity can lead to increased understanding of the requirements of movements, and finally all the above will hopefully cause a change in what and how you practice.

9 CONFIDENCE

by Jo Cooper

Confidence is an essential for competitors in all sports and at all levels. Surprisingly, the higher the level the more important it is. During the 2012 Olympics several of the commentators said - of gold-medalist of a variety of sports - that at that level 'it is all about confidence' and that it is confidence that is the difference that makes the difference between competitors who are all the best in their field. In equestrian events in which the horse gains confidence from the rider it is even more important.

When confidence is mentioned in the context of riding people usually think of riders who have lost their confidence, often after a traumatic event, and picture in their minds a rider who turns to a quivering jelly at the thought of getting on their horse. In a book titled 'Master Dressage' it seems safe to assume that the confidence that we are talking about is at a different level. It includes the confidence of knowing what needs to be done, to set achievable goals, to practise effectively and to know how to review and rehearse performance.

Competing brings with it another anxiety that is one of the most common - that of performing in front of an audience. It is interesting that the phobia of public speaking is usually listed as one of the most common phobias and when you think about it, giving a talk in public and competing in a dressage test have some similarities. In both there is often a fear of being watched, of being judged and criticised, feeling that you haven't prepared sufficiently, worrying that you might forget the test (or your words) and of not performing at one's best. There is also a fear that people will judge you as a person - rather than judge your performance - and, even worse, you may find yourself making the same mistake. If you have had a test in the past that has gone badly or that you have been criticised for, then the memory of that can add to the anxiety.

The first question is what exactly is 'confidence'. It is an abstract noun - there is no such object as confidence. It is a way of talking about a process - a verb turned into a noun - and one way to start to think about it is to think about the process that it refers to. It might be useful to think of 'confidence' as knowing what it is that you do well, knowing what you will be able to do with practice and knowing what you can't do yet.

When you consider these issues and anxieties it becomes clear that they are all to do with how you prepare for the test. In this book you are given a system that you can use when practising on your horse. This section suggests ways that you can prepare before you ride and between your schooling sessions and lessons so that your 'mind-body' system is primed to perform at your best. The 'internal' preparation that you can do includes planning and organising, reviewing past performance,and rehearsing your next steps - all of which can be done effectively off your horse. In fact this gives you an answer to the question raised about what you can do to practise between rides, especially if you are not able to ride everyday.

The 'mind body' system.

In our Western culture mind and body (and mind and brain) tend to be regarded as separate entities that can be considered without reference to each other. It is even difficult to find a way of talking about them as an integrated system - every time we refer to mind and body we are presupposing that they are separate entities. The division between mind and body rarely makes sense to anyone involved in sport, even at the lowest levels, as they know that the way they think affects how they perform. I'm choosing to refer to the mind body system as a single unit.

A simple model of how the mind body system works, and one that makes particular sense when thinking of riding, relates to how we process information. Put simply, we take in information through our senses - we see, hear, feel, smell and taste. We then process that information in the same senses. We see images in our mind's eye, we hear internal sounds and voices (including our own voice) and experience feelings. We can even conjure up smells and tastes.This is a constant process through which we develop our unique model of their world and it is this model of the world that informs our behaviour.

When we process information and build our model of the world we make finer distinctions within each sense. For example, we are influenced by the colour, brightness, shape and location of an image; the tone, pitch, volume and tempo of a sound; and the location and intensity of a feeling. The more we are aware of this process the more flexibility we have to change our experience.

As equestrians this model becomes even more interesting as it is not just the rider who functions in this way - the horse is also taking in and processing information. We have to remember that both horse and rider include each other in their models of the world and make judgements as to what is happening and how they should behave based on their experience of each other as well as other sights, sounds and even smells and tastes they experience from around them. At a competition both horse and rider are highly attuned to everything that is happening and need to maintain confidence in each other. This gives an added responsibility to the rider to maintain their confidence to support their horse.

The idea of rider and horse being an integrated system might make more sense if you think for a moment of driving a car. When you are driving do you think of yourself as separate from the car? If you imagine where your 'boundaries' are, do you think of them around you within the car - or do you extend yourself to include the car? Most experienced drivers answer this question immediately by saying that their boundaries are around the car - how else would they be able to judge distances for example. If you ask a confident experienced rider they will also answer that their boundaries extend around the horse.

A rider who is nervous and lacks confidence will most often say that their boundaries are around themselves and that they are sitting 'on' the horse. This is something you can experiment with both on and off your horse. In your mind, imagine that you are on your horse and practice changing your boundaries to include and exclude the horse and notice the effects. You can also do this when you are riding and notice the difference that it makes to your horse. When you watch an advanced rider performing at high level it becomes obvious that they and the horse almost become one.

What is your goal?

This might sound a specific question but when you think about it it contains a host of possibilities. Which goal is it talking about? It is worth thinking about your overall dressage goal. Each lesson, each schooling session, each test is a step on the way to your overall goal. It is worth considering why you have chosen dressage and what is your ultimate aim as these answers provide a context and direction for everything else that you do. The overall goal doesn't have to be about level of competition. It may be, for example, that you have chosen dressage as a means to improving your flat work and competitions are a way of measuring your success; it may be that you are an eventer and are wanting to improve your dressage results or you could be aspiring to compete in dressage at the highest level. Whatever you ultimate goal it will have an effect on how you approach each element of your practice and competition. There are no right or wrong answers here -

what you choose is up to you and you can do your best whatever your goal.

Your ultimate, longer term, goal provides a context for the decisions you make as to your immediate goal. You can apply the same thinking to any goal, large or small, and the same principles will apply. There are some basic principles that can be applied to the way that you think about your goals that apply universally but in the context of this book, let's assume that your goal is your next dressage test.

The first step is to answer the question 'what do you want?', and not 'what don't you want? It is surprising how many people when asked what they want will give answers about not making the same mistakes as last time, learning the test better, not being so worried about being watched or criticised. Just think about it. All of these answers focus on anything but the goal. The brain doesn't think in negatives and in order not to think of something it has first to think about it. You've probably heard people say 'don't think of pink elephants'! Notice what happens as you hear that - you immediately picture pink elephants and sometimes it can be difficult to get them out of your mind. If you set goals that are about 'not' doing something, what you don't want becomes your immediate focus of attention.

The answer is to think about what you do want, to be clear, concise and detailed. Say exactly what you want to achieve, when and where you want to achieve it and with whom. So for your next dressage test be clear as to which test you (and your horse!) will be doing, when and where it is and who else will be involved - including supporters, friends, instructor, trainer, and of course the judge and any officials. As you think about who else might be involved just imagine for a moment what each of them may be thinking as they attend the competition and appreciate that even if you fear someone might be critical it is often a result of their own insecurities and lack of confidence and is best not taken personally.

The next step is to frame your goal in such a way that it is possible for you and your horse to achieve it. This might sound obvious but just think for a moment. If, for example, you say that your goal is to get a specific score, or particular comments from the judge, or even to win, that really isn't within your power - all of these are dependent on the judgement of someone else. It might even be that something happens that you decide not to compete, or that something outside the arena upsets your horse and makes a high score impossible. A goal that is outside your control sets you up for the possibility of failure - something much better avoided. A more suitable goal may be to perform the test to the best of your ability, or to achieve specific movements fluently that you have found difficult before, or if you and your horse are inexperienced just doing the test irrespective of the results may be a huge achievement.

Remember that in dressage there is always an element of subjectivity. However hard they try, it is inevitable, that not all judges have the same preferences, notice the same things or mark in the same way. It is far better for you to measure yourself against your previous performance - especially to notice any improvements, and to measure your performance against your goals. Everything else is useful and interesting feedback that can help you with your next goal.

The next step is to experience achieving your goal in your mind. It is vital that you experience achieving your goal successfully - at this stage you are setting your whole system up for success. You will almost certainly have heard visualisation recommended as a tool to prepare for a competition and is one element of mental rehearsal (as mentioned elsewhere in this book). It can be even more effective to imagine that you are achieving your goal and to immerse yourself in the experience in your mind - look around you and notice what you can see, listen to all the sounds, even smells and tastes, feel the air against your skin. Then draw in your senses and notice, for example, that you can see your horse's head and ears, the angle of the neck, the movement of the shoulders. You can hear your horse's feet on the ground, perhaps the sound of your own breathing - and experience everything you feel. This will include different sorts of feelings - the feel of the saddle, the reins, your feet in the stirrups, the movement of the horse beneath you. Notice the feeling of how your body is positioned, of how you are moving, how you are using your body and all the ways that you and your horse are communicating with each other and functioning as a single unit. The more detailed your experience the better - ride the whole test in your mind paying attention to each movement and each step within it. The purpose of doing this is that as you perform the test in your mind your brain triggers micro-muscle movements in your body so that your whole system believes that the test is actually happening as you imagine it. That is the reason it is so important that you experience achieving your goal successfully - your mind body system will believe that you have already achieved it and when you arrive at the competition the more that you have been able to fully experience the test in your mind, the more familiar it will seem.

A word about learning tests - when you mentally rehearse the test using all your senses it is a significant step towards learning the test and becoming familiar with it. If you can mark out on the floor and walk the test as your are experiencing it in your mind you move your body as you will throughout the test. You will find that this helps to develop muscle memory as well as visual memory and the test begins to make much more sense to your whole mind body system.

Dealing with the downside - what could go wrong?

Having practised and mentally rehearsed the test and had the whole system experience of getting it right, you are in a much better position to explore and understand the areas that you need to improve and to pay special attention to. Now you know how things should work you are better placed to understand where things could go wrong and to make necessary adjustments. There is a simple rule when dealing with the downside. The rule is that you spend as little time as possible thinking about what went wrong previously or what might go wrong in the future - you only need to think about it for long enough to know what you are working with. Just have a quick peep at what happened and then in your mind retreat to a safe position away from the action. As you watch from this safe perspective ask yourself 'where did it start to go wrong?', go back far enough to the first point where you could have done something differently then in your mind make the change and go forward in slow motion to find out if that solves the problem. If not, rewind again and see what else you can change and then try that out too. When you have tried all the possibilities that come to mind and have a strategy to be able to perform the movements correctly, put yourself back on your horse, enter the arena and test out your new strategy. Find out how it feels and experience the detail of the changes you have made. As you continue to ride the test in your mind you may find that you have to do more fine-tuning as the adjustments that you have made may affect the way that you ride the whole test - but that is the beauty of detailed mental rehearsal. It gives you the opportunity to practise as many times as you like and in as much detail as you can.

Two key words in this book are accuracy and fluidity. Rehearsing the minutest detail in your mind is an effective way of increasing your accuracy. Remember also to focus on the transitions between movements to make sure that the accuracy of the movements includes the transitions between them and that your mental rehearsal includes attention to the fluidity of the whole test.

So - what is confidence?

In the context of 'Master Dressage' confidence is - of course - about having the confidence to ride. Much more than that, however, it is about knowing what you and your horse are capable of, being clear as to your overall goals and your specific goals. It is knowing what could go wrong, where there may have been past mistakes and to know how to deal with them so that they don't happen again. It is to have the focus and mental agility to be able to rehearse the whole test using every sense so that your mind body system believes that you have already completed the test and are fully prepared to go out and do it again.

Then you go out and enjoy the experience!

10 AN INTRODUCTION TO RIDER BIOMECHANICS

by Mary Wanless BHSI BSc

Introduction

I have been teaching riding now for over 40 years and during that time I have seen many types of rider, with many different problems that prevent them from getting the most from their riding. These riders range from the nervous novice, to competitors at different levels of the various disciplines, including professional riders. Some feel that they struggle due to lack of talent and some are talented riders who have run into a specific problem at the advanced levels.

Whatever your problem, whatever your standard, the same laws of biomechanics apply - they do not alter from the novice to the elite and act on all riders just like gravity acts on all apples! To most people, the word talent means 'She's really good at it but we don't know why.' However, talent is really about the ability to focus your attention well and the instinctive use of good biomechanics, even though the talented, instinctive rider does not know that this is what gives her that 'edge'. Talent can carry you far, but riders reach their limit when their biomechanics are not precise enough for the task in hand. As progress halts, the rider reaches a plateau and frustration and discontent are likely outcomes.

A rider who possesses the correct biomechanics will not only feel safer and more skillful, but will also have a better, clearer, relationship with her horse. If you find the 'baggage' accumulating, or even find yourself battling with your horse or calling him names, maybe it's time to take a step back. It is a brave, honest rider who does this, asking herself what her own part is in the relationship she has with her horse.

Very often when a more skilled rider gets on a pupil's horse, she can produce much better results with seemingly little effort. This is not magic; instead it is good focus and biomechanics in action. Talented riders are unconsciously versed in a system which they cannot tell you about, because to them it is as natural as breathing. In the language of social psychology, they are victims of 'Expertise Induced Amnesia'.

When an experienced driver changes gears in one fluent motion, she is not aware of the myriad of co-ordinations which must occur for this to happen. She may or may not have memories of learning and of the overwhelm and difficulty she grappled with back then. Talented riders rarely have those memories - and if they really are highly talented, they popped out of the womb with a body set up to naturally do right some of the facets that others have to learn. The traditional language of teaching is ill equipped to pass on the true A, B, Cs of riding. Instead it uses phrases like: 'Use your back', 'Use your seat', 'Sit tall', and 'stretch your leg down' . Sadly these can be interpreted in a million and one different ways and they cannot be considered a good means of communicating precise skills. Furthermore, these traditional phrases (which originally came out of the mouths of the world's more revered riders) are attempts to explain what they themselves were aware of. This means that, by definition, they are the X ,Y, Zs of riding, even though they are masquerading as its A, B, Cs. This confusion leaves many riders confused and doomed to struggle - but the problem does not lie inside them!

Virtually everyone is out there doing the best they can with the body they have and the information they have been given. Many of their problems lie outside of themselves, in the language they hear. The riding culture as a whole does not realize this and it is a costly mistake that can have a huge negative impact on learning riders.

Technique #1 - Correct Alignment

The phrase 'correct alignment' covers a number of elements within skillful riding and for this short chapter we will cover the very basics which need to be in place for a rider to have a shot at riding well.

The first question I ask myself when I assess a rider is 'If I were to take the horse out from underneath the rider, as if by magic, how would she land on the arena floor?'.

Would she land on her feet, would she fall backwards, or would she fall forwards?

In the photo above, you can see Heather Blitz, a Grand Prix dressage rider and Pan American Gold Medalist, showing correct alignment. You can see that if the horse were taken out from underneath her, she would land on her feet on the arena floor, and would then stay in that balance.

The photo below shows a participant in a 'Naked Truth of Riding' seminar, before she had been re-aligned. The lighter line is the vertical line, and the red line goes from the shoulder to the ankle bone.

Although this photo was not taken from the ideal angle of 90 degrees to the rider, you can see that she is leaning back and behind the balance point. Her feet are ahead of her backside, which is ahead of her shoulders. If we were to ask the question, 'What would happen if we took the horse away by magic?', I think it is clear that she would land on her heels and then topple back.

Skillful riding for flatwork requires a shoulder, hip, heel vertical alignment, as shown in the first photo of Heather, so that the rider remains balanced over her feet.

If the rider is already behind the balance point and not balanced over her feet, then we could use our imagination and project what would happen if we added acceleration into the picture.

Adding acceleration into the picture

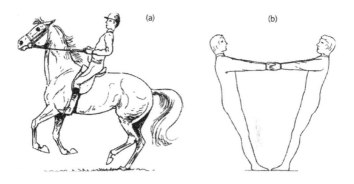

(a)   (b)

So whilst we can accept the illustration above marked (a) is rather extreme, this is what can easily happen to a rider. It's the same feeling as sitting in an airplane which is taking off. As it accelerates, you are pressed backwards into the seat. On a horse we do not have the luxury of the back of the seat to save us, so we must ourselves provide a muscular force which keeps us aligned and in place on each step. This means that without us relying on the reins, our centre of gravity must stay over the horse's centre of gravity. Pulling back on the reins (which is a force that acts from the front to the back) is the alternative to that force which acts from the back to the front. It is the much more common way in which riders save themselves.

The drawing marked (b) illustrates the energy system from the drawing (a) perfectly. Horse and rider become a counterbalancing system, as the horse pulls on the rider, the rider hangs on the horse, and neither can let go. Each one would be justified in blaming the other for pulling, but only the rider can be smart enough to find her way of out their predicament. If she brings herself into her own balance, stacked up over her feet, she forces her partner (be that horse or human) to take responsibility for himself.

Thigh at 45 degrees

When you look at the photo of Heather, you can see that her thigh is at about a 45 degree angle, halfway between vertical and horizontal. This gives the rider the best chance of maintaining her alignment. If the stirrups are too long and the thigh too vertical, then the rider will be reaching into her stirrups. Have a look at some of the world's top riders and you will find that their thighs rarely get longer than 40 degrees to vertical (i.e. slightly longer than I recommend for learning riders).

It will probably take a friend, or a mirror, to help you set yourself up in the correct shoulder, hip, heel alignment with a 45 degree thigh, but this is the very basis from which I work. Without this alignment further progress is difficult and the rider is very likely to get stuck on a plateau. Be prepared to put your stirrups up (or possibly down) to get the correct angle AND be prepared for the fact that this may well feel very strange to your body. Most people fail to make the progress they deserve because they are put off at how strange and different they will have to feel in order to make the changes they need.

To improve - which means to change - we have to do something different to what we are doing now. And change can feel very weird indeed. Usually the corrections I make to riders do not involve doing more or less of something they are currently doing, but involve doing something really different! Few people are prepared for this!

Technique #2 - Neutral Spine

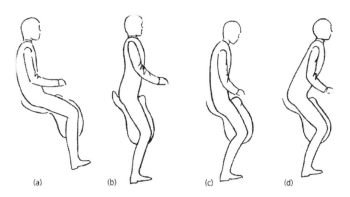

(a)   (b)   (c)   (d)

Neutral spine is the ideal way of sitting, in which the rider's spinal curves are balanced and her seat bones point down. The rider is neither hollow-backed, which makes her seat bones point backwards, nor round-backed which makes them point forwards. In this position the spine is best placed to withstand the forces acting on it and the rider can stabilize her lumbar spine so that she does not 'wiggle in the middle'. Many riders who have back pain become pain free once they discover how to ride in neutral spine. The illustration above shows some of the different ways in which a rider can lose neutral spine.

a) Round backed and leaning back into the 'arm chair seat', with the rider sitting on her pockets and her seat bones pointing forwards.

b) Hollow backed, with rider sitting on her fork, her seat bones pointing backwards, and the stomach sucked in.

c) Round backed, pulling in the stomach with the seat bones pointing forwards, albeit less than in a).

d) Seat bones pointing backwards and tipped forward,

with the rider folding at the hip towards jumping position.

A good way for you to see which way your seats bones point, is to find a firm chair, and sit on your hands with your palms facing up, so you can feel your seat bones. Then start to experiment by hollowing your back and then rounding your back, gradually reducing the extremes until you find the neutral place which makes your seat bones point straight down.

At the 'Naked Truth of Riding' symposium, Heather demonstrated how she looked before she started working with me many years ago. You can see, in the photo below, that she was not in neutral spine: she leant back, hollowed her back, and had her stirrups far too long! As she said 'I thought this was what you were supposed to do!'

Technique #3 - Core Strength

This was the first thing I discovered that really made a difference when I came back to riding after giving up in despair and frustration. I began again with a beginner's mind - a mind which started noticing the cause and effect interactions between horse and rider, and had no other agenda about how it ought to be, or what I should be doing.

I had to train and ride out a very speedy horse, who liked to jog. I was gradually able to piece together how, using core strength, I was able to control the tempo of the horse's footsteps and not get jiggled around by his movements. This also involved staying in the correct alignment so that I did not become the water skier to his motor boat. Whenever I lost it, I would pull, he would pull, and he just kept jogging. When I found it, I could slow his legs and choose to remain in walk or a slow trot without pulling at all. I am eternally grateful to that horse, whose patterns were so extreme!

Good riders sit really still, looking like a carousel pole growing out of the horses back. They are undisturbed by the horse's antics and are in control of their bodies. I called this new found skill and tone 'bearing down'. We now also use the terms 'bear forward' and 'bear out', depending on which makes most sense to the rider.

If you clear your throat (do it now) you will realize how your abdominal muscles engage as you do so. This is bearing down, and good riders do it continually. (Try this again as you sit in your chair, and then hold the muscle used which enabled you to do it. Can you breathe in and out and still do it?) Most riders almost die of shock when I teach them this, because it feels so alien and so difficult to do. But this is how skilled riders access the core strength that helps to stabilize them. It is easier, however, when you are actually riding, since it is designed for action. If you push a broom away from you when sweeping, you naturally bear down. The safest way to lift heavy weights is to bend your knees and bear down, rather than leaning over whilst pulling your stomach in.

Bearing down often conflicts with the theory a rider has learned — for if she has been trying to 'grow up tall' she will have pulled her stomach in during the process. She then utilises a breathing pattern which I call 'breathing up' - lifting her chest, ribs, and shoulders on every in-breath. Nervous riders instinctively do this and many other people do it because the theory they have heard convinces them that it must be the right way. But bearing down requires 'breathing down', in which every in-breath is drawn downwards, filling out the lower ribs and belly much more than the upper chest. Singers, runners, and people who have played wind instruments already know how to do this and they bring a tremendous advantage to their riding.

I have several free videos which help explain some of these concepts, these will be available on the resources page being put together by Peter.

11 PHYSIOTHERAPY

by

Sue Palmer MCSP

Since you are reading this book, it is automatically assumed that you are passionate about the health and well being of your horse. It is my belief that massage is something that we can all offer to our horses, and I wrote the book and DVD 'Horse Massage for Horse Owners' to encourage all horse owners to 'have a go' with confidence and enjoyment. First of all the horses love it (i.e. you can have a better relationship with your horse!), and secondly massage can reduce the risk of injury, pain or stiffness, improve performance (i.e. ride more beautiful tests and get higher marks!), and above all, help maintain health and wellbeing. Remember, you can massage your own horse on a regular basis, all you need is time, guidance, and a little practice.

'Massage is the practice of applying structured or unstructured pressure, tension, motion, or vibration — manually or with mechanical aids — to the soft tissues of the body, including muscles, connective tissue, tendons, ligaments, joints and lymphatic vessels to achieve a beneficial response.' (Wikipedia). Anyone can learn to massage their own horse. You don't need any qualifications or prior experience, or to be a particular type of person. Massage can be as gentle or as firm as you choose it to be, there is a type of massage to suit every person and every horse.

There is plenty of evidence to support massage as a therapeutic modality. In the human field, massage has been shown many times to be effective, especially when combined with exercise and advice. A study published in the Equine Veterinary Journal (and reported on in the Horse and Hound) demonstrated the effectiveness of equine massage for decreasing pain.

Massage is something you can get started on straight away. A kind of stroking technique called effleurage is the basis of many forms of massage. It's easy to learn, so why not have a go with your own horse? Decide on the area that you want to massage, perhaps the back muscles in the area under the saddle. Place the palm of your hand on the horse at the front of this area, and apply some pressure, the majority of it through the heel of your hand. Use a level of pressure that feels comfortable to you. Keeping the pressure on, slide your hand along the area you've chosen to massage. Feel the skin and muscles rippling along in front of your hand like a wave.

Photo 5 – Applying the palm of your hand

If your horse flinches away from the pressure, it might be that you've surprised him, or it might be that he's sore in which case you should contact a professional to assess him (your vet or Chartered Veterinary Physiotherapist is a good place to start). You should be able to massage the back muscles without causing pain, applying up to as much pressure as you would use to dent a football, as long as you press gradually rather than suddenly. You don't need to work this hard though to be of benefit to your horse. Practise on your own arm and see how lightly you can press and yet still feel an effect. Each person and each horse will have a level of pressure that they prefer, experiment to find what's right for you and your horse.

Another common technique is cupping, which is great for encouraging circulation to an area, and so can be important for providing energy to the muscles when warming up and encouraging lymphatic drainage during the cooling down process. Cup your hand so that the edges of your hand (little finger, tips of fingers, thumbs and heel of hand) comes into contact with the horse, trapping air within the palm of your hand. Working with both hands alternately in a steady rhythm, clap your hands against the muscle of the horse. Start very gently, and look for the ripples of skin and muscle that spread out from the area you connect with. A light touch is often more effective than a heavy hand, but each horse is an individual, so use a level of pressure that suits both you and your horse. This technique is similar to the 'strapping' that horses used to receive every day from their grooms (and still do in some of the best yards). You can use it anywhere that is muscular, for example over the quarters or the back muscles, but it could be painful if you use it over bony areas, for example the false hip (tuber coxae) or the top of the back (dorsal spinous processes).

It can be difficult deciding where to massage your horse, and in what direction to work. Developing a routine can improve your confidence and enjoyment in massaging your horse. It might help to remember that you are massaging the muscles that are underneath the skin, and to keep your focus on those rather than the skin and hair that your hand is touching. This means that it doesn't matter if you massage in the direction of, or against the hair, because it's the not the hair you're massaging! If you've had a professional work with your horse, you may have an idea of where he's sore or tight, and you can concentrate on that area. However, try to develop a routine that covers the whole body. Start gently with the neck, work over the shoulders, down into the girth area and along the back, and then across the quarters. When you get it right your horse will relax, and the massage will be an enjoyable experience for both you and your horse.

There are many clues that suggest your horse might benefit from massage or physical therapy. For example, if your horse flinches away from the brush, it is almost certain that he has some sore areas. If he is more difficult to work on one rein than the other, then the problem is more likely to be physical than behavioural (although it could be that you have the physical restriction rather than your horse!). If your horse has suddenly changed in his behaviour, for example he starts napping when he has previously enjoyed hacking out, then consider whether there might be a physical cause. These and many more are examples that might encourage you to try massaging to relieve soreness or tightness, or to call a professional to advise you how you could best help your horse.

Physiotherapy on animals (which in this case includes all kinds of manipulative therapy) is regulated by the Veterinary Surgeons Act 1966. This means that a therapist treating your horse should always have permission from your vet. If they don't ask for your vet's details, or ask you to contact the vet yourself, perhaps you might question why. There are many equine therapists available, and it can be difficult to know who to trust. Members of the Association of Chartered Physiotherapists in Animal Therapy are qualified to treat humans, and have trained further to qualify to treat animals. You can find your local Chartered Veterinary Physiotherapist at www.acpat.co.uk.

Massage is beneficial for both you and your horse. It allows you to give something back in return for all that your horse gives you. You can monitor his physical wellbeing and recognise better when to call a professional to treat him. You can help to reduce pain and stiffness, and maintain good health. The more comfortable your horse is, the better his behaviour and / or performance is likely to be, and the more opportunities you will have to reward him, thus developing a positive cycle of further improved behaviour and / or performance. Massage is something that can be achieved and enjoyed by everyone.

All in all, learning to massage your horse is a great idea! The Horse Massage for Horse Owners Book and DVD is detailed yet easy to follow, teaching you a complete massage routine that you can use with your horse. You can find out more at www.thehorsephysio.co.uk.

Sue Palmer MCSP, Chartered Veterinary Physiotherapist, BHSAI, Equine Behaviourist (Intelligent Horsemanship Recommended Associate, holder of the Monty Roberts Preliminary Certificate in Horsemanship)

www.thehorsephysio.co.uk

12 YOUR NEXT STEPS

Congratulations you have made it through the book to the end! I hope I have given you lots to think about and hopefully enlightened you on some aspects of dressage training and riding.

Now that you are here, you may be bubbling with ideas and ready to rock and roll, or you may be wondering what you should tackle first. With so much information it can be confusing to know where to start.

I think the first thing you can do, if you are at all worried about your own skill set, is to have a look at the resources section which contains a lot of links to videos and articles which can help. Also have a look at the recommended reading section too, some of the books listed will skyrocket your understanding of riding skills.

After that, I would spend some time in the review. Anytime you take a journey, its fine knowing where you want to get to, but first of all you need to know where you are currently at! Go through the checklists, make notes of anywhere in the book where you said "Yes that's me" and write it all down. The goal is to do the very best you can do, for yourself and your horse. So lets take it seriously by setting aside a good hour to do an initial review of where things stand. Gather up your score sheets if you have any and make notes on those too.

Be honest with yourself more than anything else. By explicitly stating your problems, weaknesses and issues you will make fast progress. Try to sort out if the problems are to do with your riding, with your expectations of your horse or through a lack of understanding.

After you have done a thorough review you will need to decide what it is you are going to do about it. This is quite an important stage and I suggest you pick the largest problem you have to tackle first. This could be "struggling to stay on the bit", "can't keep my horse straight", "horses quarters in canter", "can't position my horse well in half pass", "find getting energy a problem" – whatever it is this should be the "difference that makes the difference". What is the one thing for you that would make the biggest impact to your dressage scores and your enjoyment of riding?

You can often answer this question easily by saying to yourself "If only my horse would just....". Just fill in the dots for yourself and you will almost always have the answer to the thing which bugs you the most. After you have your answer I hope you have an idea what to do next. You may need to improve you accuracy, your fluidity, your understanding, perhaps start to focus on practicing more effectively – I think you can see why I picked the 5 step structure for training!

Riding is a very expensive hobby, or sport and we all have a range of financial means. For some of us, getting access to a coach may be financially or logistically impossible. If this is the case for you, then certain of the books I have mentioned will help, but make sure you take up the offer of the free months access to the weekly webinars that I am holding. This means you will get access to 4 webinars. Each webinar will cover different topics, with plenty of time for you to ask questions of me or the expert that I have invited along to speak with me. I can't think of any books that will give you that kind of after sales support!

You can always write to me too and I will do my best to answer questions, however I cannot guarantee a response due to time limitations, hence why I urge you to attend the webinars. If there is ONE thing I would love to hear from you about, is how you got down to the task of review and what you came up with? Write to me and let me know what your review revealed combined with what I have taught in the book.

In the resources section I have put a link to a web page

where you can post the results of your review. I will keep checking the page and making comments where I can.

Dressage is an amazing game! Its fun, rewarding and hard work. It keeps you fit, it engages your brain and brings you a whole new appreciation for your horse. Dressage requires of you the things you do not naturally have. If you are impulsive, you will need to learn to be patient. If you are somewhat timid, you will need to take more command of the situation. If you are highly strung you will need to school your reactions and develop an inner calmness. When riding well it can feel like you are on a knifes edge, you have a narrow path to walk of power and control with you as the peaceful centre.

Let your horse be your guide because, as a rule, horses are out to please you. Perhaps they can be a little wily as they seem to get away with doing just the right amount of work needed but there is no malice. Your horse will tell you when you need to get help, to learn more, to increase your skill set. The moment things become frustrating, tense, difficult, and there seems nothing you can do, it is usually your horse saying "Hey you, you aren't doing it right!" – a lot of people would think this a tough pill to swallow, but I know horse people – we love our horses, we devote huge amounts of our time to them and beyond all else we want the very best for them.

Peter Dove

13 YOUR QUESTIONS

In this chapter I answer questions posted to me by the fans of my Facebook page over at

http://facebook.com/MasterDressage

Q : Is it better to come in at A on the rein that you will be turning on at C?

A : One should come in on the rein which produces the best turn and which gets you on the centre line straightest. After all, you will have to travel up the centre line straight - so the rein you come in on shouldn't have that much effect on the turn at C.

Q : I had a comment about my horse in the last test, it said he was dragging his toes. He is only 5 and this was his 2nd test.

A : I find this sort of thing, if it's just a laziness, flexion or a strength issue, to be solved through trotting poles and then slightly raised trotting poles. It teaches the horse to pick its feet up and develop a little extra flexion in its hocks.

Q : In counter canter, do you flex the horses neck in the direction your going, counter flexion or straightness?

A : In Counter Canter you should maintain the bend suited to the canter. So, if you are in canter-left, you should remain bent to the left, even if you are on the right rein.

Q : When a test requires you to enter and continue down the centre line without a halt, should you "ignore" the judge or should you give them a "smile and nod" approximately at G? I've always done the latter as I feel it's more correct and a smile is the best was to evaporate tension. Also we have a super local judge, but soon I will need to broaden our horizons, so would value your opinion. Thanks.

A : I tend to completely ignore them ☺ on that first centre line, unless I have enough brain space to hold a general bright smile. I wait until the end to make eye contact and unleash my charm! Normally though I just don't have enough brain space to acknowledge them at the start.

Q : How can we get a 10 in free walk on a long rein? I've had comments that she's not stretching down enough, surely a free walk is exactly that and should not be forced that much? What aids should I be giving and where should she be? Thanks. X

A : I think the main things that free walk on a long rein shows is that the horse is always seeking the contact, that the horse is supple over its back and it can march forwards whilst doing it. It shows suppleness and relaxation over the entire top line and a complete willingness to reach towards the riders hand and seek the contact. My daughter just did a test today and got a 8. For her to get a 10, the horse would have needed to be more active, a little straighter and have a neater and quicker transition from free walk to medium walk (She took her time and was still in free a little after the marker). The stretching down element is an extremely important proof of correct work.

Q : (Follow on from above) So we should not give the rein away? That we should maintain some contact for them to work down into? Very interesting about the transitions!

A : That's correct, it's free walk on a long rein, not loose rein. You need to train your horse to naturally follow the contact of the rein and stretch over its back, so as you lengthen the rein gradually the horse maintains contact. When training the horse to do this movement, I slightly lighten my seat by tipping forwards a little to encourage the back to come up.

Q : In the Grand Prix canter half-pass zig-zag, the sequence is said to be 3-6-6-6-3-change. Why do people do so many variations of stride in the final 3 stride and not get marked lower than a competitor who actually does 3 strides?

A : I focus on teaching intro to elementary, however I know that there are a lot of elements which come together to qualify a score and making a mistake in that last element of the sequence with everything performed smoothly, will always beat someone doing the sequence accurately but with poor changes and poor form. For instance, changes being late behind, horse swinging its quarters in the change, changes being croup high etc.

Q : When riding corners I have been told to make it an arc of a circle. Then the higher the level, the smaller the circle. So my question is, do you ever ride the corners as an actual 90 degree turn? Or is that only when the test asks for one, e.g turn on to centreline at A.

A : Its always a quarter circle - any right angled turn is made up from a turn on a quarter circle - it just gets smaller the more advanced you get.

Q : What are the judges looking for in medium trot at novice level? I lengthen the frame, lengthen the steps without increasing the rhythm but get bad marks - seems like they want more of extended type trot..

A : Without seeing your test I can't say. When the judge looks at their sheet, it often gives guidance as to what to look for. Ground cover is one, and the horse should over track clearly showing it is covering more ground. They also want to see that the horse can move in and out of lengthening easily without losing balance.

Q : How much bend should there be in half pass? I seem to get comments which ask for less at times and then some that ask for more! Also seems to be relevant in the shoulder in movement.

A : I think sometimes disparity in comments can come from viewing angles. The horse should be slightly bent around the inside leg. Have a look at some of Charlotte Dujardin's tests on YouTube and check out the bend there.

Q : How do you get a heavy on the bit horse off the forehand without pulling on the rein?

A : This can be a bit tricky to solve depending on your skill level because solving this issue requires that you can use your leg and control the tempo of the horse. Often an instructor will say, you use your leg to engage the hind legs, however most people will find that this speeds up the horse and causes it to be more on the forehand. This kind of fix is really a rider biomechanics question, because you need to know what the rider is doing to the horse and what the horse is doing to the rider before you can offer a solution.

Q : What I would like to know is when is really the best time to cue the horse for the transition, would it be just before the letter marker or right at it??? Just trying to see what the judges would be looking for on the cues.

A : It actually depends on the ability of your horse, though most horses, even top level horses, need a moment to receive the instruction and act! So always slightly before, so that when you make the transition your shoulders are at the marker. I am always wary of too much preparation for downward transitions, or you end up with a wind down trot, so the transition should be fairly clean. I work hard not to transmit the transition too early and continue riding towards the marker as if I had no intention of making a transition, then just before ask.

Q : How do you keep your horse relaxed and supple in the ring? Mine warms up beautifully but as soon as he's in the ring I have no control! Any help/tips would be much appreciated, thank you

A : It's actually hard to say without seeing but I can certainly tell you typical problems. One main issue is that people breathe less well when under stress, this leads to lack of oxygen and you just generally have reduced access to your core strength and skill set than you otherwise would - so just make an extra effort to focus on it. The other thing to have a look at, perhaps using video, is do you ride any differently when you get in the ring? Often we say things to ourselves like "Right! Let's get this show on the road!" or "Come on horse we have a job to do" and we place additional pressure on ourselves and the horse that just were not there in the warm up, in addition to riding differently.

Q : I am riding a highly trained Appaloosa gelding, he responds well to my leg and seat as his trot is quite smooth but I just had a clinic with him and the lady told me he's stiff as a 2x6 in walking and trotting and he changes his tempo a lot. Our first show is soon, how do I get his walk bigger without going into the trot? How do I get his trot bigger without running him?

A : In order to create impulsion, shorten or lengthen a stride, we must have tempo control. We must be able to use our leg, and have it mean more than 'move your legs quicker'. The first step is to learn to 'plug in' in walk and be able to control the tempo through your seat bones. There is a great video by Mary Wanless which teaches this. I will provide a list of resources on my website.

Q : How can I ride the perfect square halt?
A : Riding a square halt is both down to your technique

in halting, which is a product of how good your biomechanics are for halts and part to do with the natural inclination of the horse. Some horses just halt squarely more naturally. However I would say that you need to learn exactly what it feels like when each of your horses hind legs are backwards or forwards. Have a friend call out as you walk, which hind leg is forward or back in the walk and as you halt, see if you can guess whether he is square or which hind leg is left behind. Try to feel if one side is dropped away, how your seat bones and pelvis feel and so on. Learning the skill of halting squarely takes a lot of time and experimentation on your behalf but it is well worth the investment of time and energy as this will always pay dividends on the next horse you have to train.

Q : I had a serious accident on a riding school horse that decided to buck me off onto a fence post when I asked it to canter . As a result of the accident the right side of my cheek was seriously injured and was paralysed. (The actual aim of the lesson was to develop my confidence , not good result) since then till now I can't bring my own horse into a relaxed strike off into canter and it takes a good few strides for him to relax without power housing round the arena ....what can I do to relax my mind and believe in myself to do it which in turn should chill him?

A : Sorry about the accident. It might be worth having him ridden by someone else, just to see who is the chicken and who is the egg in this scenario. And it may just be that if you have a rider you trust to school him, that they can teach him not to rush after the strike off. You should also check how you sit when you ask for the canter, perhaps you sit too far back, or perhaps land a little heavy. One of the best teachers I know for learning how to sit still and 'plug in' is Mary Wanless. I believe she posted a video on her page about plugging in.

How good is your sitting trot? You might gain that extra little bit of control if you can do this in sitting trot before you ask.

Q : How do I give and retake the reins, I always seem to get low marks for it?

A : A lot of people seem to be doing the give and retake by raising their hands forward and up, which ends up not showing the give at all well. Your hand should move towards the horse's mouth and create a loop in the rein. The loop in the rein is the important part, it shows the horse is maintaining his own balance and doesn't just dive off onto your hand, or change his carriage the moment there is no contact.

Q : Would you teach a young horse shoulder in or half pass first? To me not knowing a great deal about dressage they seem one and the same thing, my horse and I are learning together so any help is appreciated.

A : Would teach shoulder-in first. The reason is that half-pass requires much more suppleness from the horse and much more lateral stepping.

Q : What is the correct way to teach a horse to reinback. My boy just doesn't get it. Plants his feet and hollots his back. He happily does it when I stand in front of him and touch his chest and say back, getting him to understand the verbal cue.

A : I would look at the ground work offered by Andrew McLean - because the queue for your horse to rein back should not be a push on the chest, but begin with rein contact, in combination with leg aids. Andrews work teaches the horse to halt from the lightest touch. Essentially Andrews work is the closest way of emulating a person riding the horse and do a great job in making the riders life easier.

Q : My mare is 23 years old and still going strong. She has given me the dressage bug and at some point in the future I want to get another younger horse once she retires whenever that may be.

What would you say the most important things are to look for in a horse to progress onto the higher levels of dressage? Also would you pin point a specific breed for this as most horses at the higher levels are warmbloods.

A : I don't prefer a specific breed, but trainability is one aspect, then you should be looking at conformation. You need to make sure it moves straight, you need to assess the quality of its paces, does it clearly over track in walk, in trot is there a good spring to its trot, does it flex well at the hocks and so on. Getting some good information on gait analysis or conformation will help.

Q : How do you get the horse to reach for the bit?

A: I recommend that you start with ground work, either through lungeing or through the work of Andrew McLean. I also explain in great detail how to do free walk on a long rein, or as said in USEF or FIDE, stretching on a long rein. This is a great exercise to teach your horse to seek the contact.

Q : My daughter has just come off lead and has done a handful of walk trot. She has a tendency to drop the outside contact on left rein so pony falls out and we then have 'steering issues' any suggestions of how I can help her with this.

A : I would ask her to give you a number from 1 to 10 on how much she is focusing on the outside rein contact as she makes the transition. 10 would be totally focused and 1 would be totally forgot about it. Each time ask her for a number. Just the exercise itself should help her stay more focused and aware.

14 LEARNING RESOURCES

It is always annoying having a whole list of internet links inside a book. There is the inevitable typos from the author, and pages tend to go offline. To solve this from happening, I am just going to leave you with one link, to the resources page on my website. This page will contain all the other links. You can even get there by going to my website and clicking the resources menu.

http://masterdressage.co.uk/resources/

At the back of this book, there are a few pages of adverts from people I can recommend. They offer services and products which will not only improve your riding but also improve the wellbeing of your horse.

In general you should certainly look into the works of Mary Wanless BHSI, she is an expert on Rider Biomechanics, and can help you learn the 'how' of talented riding. She has quite a few books, videos and online training resources as well as residential clinics.

I am available for clinics, lectures and demonstrations, just go to my website and contact me via there. You should also check out the offer in the middle of the book which gives you a free months access to weekly webinars with myself and other experts, who will not only teach you new subjects but who can also answer any questions you have.

You should also get yourself out to some well run practice days, its minimum stress and you will learn a lot.

Peter Dove

SPECIAL OFFER

As a thank you for purchasing this book, I offering a whole months worth of weekly webinars absolutely free. By following the link below you will be able to sign up for a months trial of the Master Dressage Lectures. As a member you will be able to watch previous recorded lectures and get details for accessing the live webinars each week.

During each webinar you will be able to get answers to your own questions from either myself or to the guest speaker. I will be inviting on other equestrian experts to help out, so the topics will be varied and designed to round out our equestrian knowledge.

Follow the link below and sign up, I'm really looking forward to helping you out on the webinars and hearing how you are getting on with your schooling and riding.

http://masterdressage.co.uk/webinar/

Members of the Master Dressage Lectures also get access to free training videos, articles and will be able to access a forum where you can post videos and pictures asking for advise and support.

Peter Dove

15 READING LIST

There is somewhat of a theme here for the reading list, but I can't really recommend many other books because they simply assume the rider knows how to do so many things already. This is not because the books are bad, but they provide advice for which the rider is, as yet, too unskilled to implement well. Once the rider has some good biomechanics in place, they have a chance at implementing the instructions found in these other books.

For instance, I have a copy of "Training The Young Horse: The first two years by Anthony Crossley". It was one of the first books I ever bought on horses. I look at it now and realise, way back when I bought it, I had none of the skills to be able to implement what was being taught, nor was I discerning enough to be able to reject or accept the advice offered. I still have the copy on my desk and it makes an interesting read.

Ride With Your Mind (The Natural Rider) by Mary Wanless. This book changed my riding and my life. It's quite a technical read but I loved it and it changed me forever.

Ride With Your Mind Essentials by Mary Wanless. This book is a much more user friendly introduction to rider biomechanics complete with excellent illustrations.

Dressage Rulebooks! Whatever organisation you are riding with, even if you are just doing unaffiliated/riding club/schooling shows, you should get the appropriate dressage rulebook from your countries dressage body. Some of them are very detailed and have great information on what they are looking for from the rider and horse.

Horse Massage for Horse Owners by Sue Palmer. This is a great book for it gives us the power to help our horses through massage. Not only do you learn how to reduce stiffness in your horse, but it helps bring you closer to your horse and develop a better relationship.

Ride With Your Mind Masterclass by Mary Wanless. Though this book is out of print, it can still be bought second hand. It contains a number of lessons with pupils, all on different subjects with photographs illustrating the different issues with which the pupils struggled. It is exactly because you get to see many people with different problems, you find yourself able to identify with them. Check it out on amazon, it has some lovely reviews.

Ride With Your Mind Clinic by Mary Wanless. I really love this book, Mary takes Grand Prix rider Heather Blitz as the model for demonstrating good rider biomechanics and then gives lessons to other students using before and after photos showing how to get closer to the previously explained model.

Self-Discipline – No Excuses by Brian Tracy – This is an eye opener of a book on responsibility, self-discipline, goal setting and more. Well worth reading and will improve your life!

The Talent Code by Daniel Coyle – This is the book that will inspire you to new learning and to realise that you don't need 'talent' to get a very long way in any sphere of learning.

THANKS

No book would be complete without a thank you page. At least no book of mine! There are so many people who helped to get this book out, who gave encouragement, who gave me editing assistance and who have over the period I have known them enriched my knowledge and life.

I'd like to thank my wife Emma Dove, and my children Milly & Edward Dove for all their support and encouragement and for putting up with Dad being locked away in his office for so long. Also thanks again to Milly for being brave enough to have her photos put into the book.

I'd like to thank Mary Wanless without whom this would have never happened. Though I think no power on earth would have prevented me discovering her teaching!

Thank you very much to those that helped editing the book, among them were Mary Wanless, Linda Yeardley, Michael Clark, Milly Dove and many others who checked out snippets from the book. A special mention also to Karin Major who has a very sharp eye and found many more inconsistencies. In case any typos or grammatical errors slip through, they are completely resolved of any error – a lot of writing had to happen away from their eagle eyes too!

Thanks goes also to Janet Holimon Stone who pointed out that free walk on a long rein means different things depending on whether you are working under British Dressage rules or USEF/FEI. The USEF/FEI version is stretching on a long rein!

I'd like to thank Patricia Reszetylo for challenging me

on the cover formatting.

Finally I would like to add a word of thanks to Iliah Borg who helped me through a pretty rough time in my life a long time ago, he gave selflessly of his wisdom and time. Thank you Iliah.

Peter Dove has been riding, teaching and learning dressage for over 25 years. In the 15 years he has been at East Soley EC2000 he has judged and taught combined, some 9000 riders competing at intro to elementary level and beyond. Over the 15 years he has developed systematics ways of explaining how to improve results competing at dressage.

Peter is taught by Mary Wanless BHSI and considers her teachings of rider biomechanics to be one of the main keys to success at all levels of riding and is forever in her debt for all she has taught.

Peter is also a professional computer programmer, photographer and magician. He lives in Chilton Foliat in the UK, married to Emma Dove with two beautiful children Milly and Edward. He is currently studying for his Maths degree with the open university.

On The Bit Lecture Series

Renowned rider biomechanics coach, Mary Wanless BHSI BSc, author of the Ride With Your Mind books and DVDs held a series of Webinars going into detail about getting your horse 'On The Bit' and into the seeking reflexes.

All 6 lectures are now recorded and available for viewing.

Lecture 1 On The Bit – The Seeking Reflexes
Lecture 2 On The Bit – 3 Dimensions (i.e. the rider's task in the planes of up/down, back/front, side/side)
Lecture 3 On The Bit – The Mental Problem
Lecture 4 On The Bit – Troubleshooting – common horse problems
Lecture 5 On The Bit – What can prevent it from working?
Lecture 6 On The Bit – Through gaits and transitions

Plus you get supporting videos for each lecture and other goodies along the way. At only £10 per lecture it's way more value than a lesson, plus you get actionable steps to take away from each lecture to try on your horse. Once your payment has been made you will be directed to your membership area where you can watch all 6 webinars and their supporting videos.

For Booking and More Information Go To

https://theskillfulrider.com

Peter Dove

The Naked Truth Of Riding DVD Set

These DVDs are unique in their way of combining rider biomechanics and 'reactivity training'. Used together, these paradigms eat into the catch 22 that 'until the horse goes right the rider cannot sit right and until the rider sits right the horse cannot go right.' The results are profound, as illustrated in the changes made by the riders' themselves, and within Heather Blitz's riding and commentary.

DVD 1 is a talk given my Mary Wanless on Language and Learning, explaining why elite riders cannot describe their skill accurately in words and why riders so often get stuck on a plateau. Mary offers suggestions for ways of learning that ensure continual progress.

DVD 2 works in the arena with a group of 4 club level riders. After assessing and realigning the riders and then doing some teaching to confirm those changes, Heather then rides 2 of the horses.

DVD 3 works in the arena with a group of 3 slightly more advanced riders, assessing and realigning them and then doing some teaching before Heather rides 2 of the horses.

DVD 4 works in the arena with 2 more advanced riders and again after realigning and teaching, Heather rides both horses.

The descriptions used by both Mary and Heather, the analysis of the issues presented, and the changes in the horses, present some fascinating new ways of thinking that speak for themselves.

Go to the product tab from www.mary-wanless.com to see more about this groundbreaking DVD set.

Peter Dove

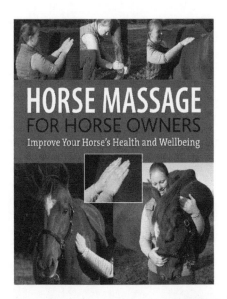

Sue Palmer MCSP

Chartered Veterinary Physiotherapist
(ACPAT Category A)

Equine Behaviourist
*(Intelligent Horsemanship Recommended Associate, holder of
the Monty Roberts Preliminary Certificate in Horsemanship)*

BHSAI

www.thehorsephysio.co.uk

Lindsay Jenkins

International Grand Prix Rider
British Dressage List 1 Judge
FEI 3/4*Event Judge
Accredited Coach with British Dressage

Dressage & Training

At Kintbury Park Farm there are horses at all levels of training, from young horses just beginning their career, up to advanced horses competing at international level.

Horses can be taken for short or long term training at all levels and packages can be planned to suit the horse, the rider and the pocket!

As a trainer, Lindsay has helped coach riders to reach Junior and Young Rider medal-winning Eventing teams, as well as helping International Senior Riders get to grips with flying changes and lateral work required at the more advanced eventing levels.

At present Lindsay teaches and trains riders of all levels and abilities up to Prix St Georges / Intermediate level.

Our International arena is an excellent venue to teach both yourself and your horse to the highest dressage levels.

Teaching is on a one-to-one basis with Lindsay.
Please call to arrange your lesson.

Lessons cost : £45.00 per 40 minute session with own horse
£65.00 per 40 minute session with the schoolmaster

www.lindsayjenkins.co.uk

Kintbury Park Farm, Kintbury, Hungerford, Berkshire RG17 9XA
Telephone: 01488 658585
Fax: 01488 657300
Email us: lindsay@lindsayjenkins.co.uk

Peter Dove

PERFORMANCE AND CONFIDENCE COACHING

Do you need help to increase your motivation, overcome performance anxiety, enhance your pre-test preparation or boost your confidence in yourself and in your performance?

Jo Cooper is a qualified and experienced practitioner who specialises in working with equestrians and other sports people to enhance their performance. She has worked with thousands of riders and her clients include every level of rider from experienced riders looking for competitive edge to beginners who need to boost their confidence.

She also helps people to resolve post traumatic stress and often works with riders who have had traumatic and scary experiences both on and off their horses.

Jo works mainly by telephone as well as face-to-face and can be available for last minute assistance prior to, and even during, competitions. If you are interested in arranging a group confidence workshop or an equestrian NLP event Jo will be happy to arrange this with you. You can read much more at www.equestrianconfidence.com

Jo has developed her unique way of working over a number of years. Her background is in NLP (Neuro-Linguistic Programming) —the basis of much sports psychology—which she first encountered NLP in the mid 80s. In 1998 was one of a handful of people in the UK certified as a Master Trainer by Dr Richard Bandler, co-founder of NLP. She was also one of the first people in the UK to train extensively with Dr Roger Callahan, founder of TFT, a technique that involves tapping on acupressure points to resolve psychological and emotional issues and which is becoming increasingly well-known. Having worked with thousands of riders over the past 15 years Jo is known for her ability to understand the problems faced by riders and to help riders to overcome them. Her work has featured in The Times, Your Horse, Horse and The Field magazines as well as local media and on TV and radio.

Jo Cooper
www.equestrianconfidence.com

Peter Dove

HAWES BORDAS

We are a team aiming and working in the same way, with our horses. We very much believe in the classical principles of working horses biomechanically correctly, so allowing forward, natural motion, that then just simply is enhanced with gymnastic exercises.

Our principles are echoed when training/coaching riders too. If one moves with ease, one can move happily and with comfort, and what's best is the horse is so much more appreciative and understanding of your aids.

We met when in france, at the prestigious l'Ecole National d'Equitation, training with the Cadre Noir in Saumur. Demelza was taking her training exams on the international course, having been accepted by the strict entrance procedures and Nicolas was finishing his high level coaching and training exams after 3 years of hard study within the equine industry.

Demelza, having finished her time in France, then started her own successful dressage training yard in Buckinghamshire on her parents Farm. Nicolas meanwhile, worked with Irish team eventer Mark Kyle, as well as training Marks pupils to finish their equine exams. A year was also spent with the UK's greatest eventer Mr William Fox-Pitt.

Our skills now combine to give a great package as we cover so many bases. Demelza's top showing career as a young rider, and natural education, as well as tough training in Germany and France, combine with Nicolas's methodical training and pedagogy, and experience at some of the greatest competitions in the world, including the London Olympics in 2012.

High level care and management meet, natural awareness and affinity to create efficient and effective, principled training and welfare.

www.hawesbordas.com

Peter Dove

THE NEXT PROJECT

Edward Dove riding "Thordale Phyllis SPSBS" with his ever helpful sister Milly Dove.

Peter Dove

Peter Dove

Printed in Great Britain
by Amazon.co.uk, Ltd.,
Marston Gate.